Always in My Heart

PET CHAPLAIN LEARNING SERIES • VOLUME 2

Always in My Heart
Coping Creatively with Pet Loss

Rob Gierka, EdD
Karen Duke

Copyright © 2026 by Rob Gierka and Karen Duke. All rights reserved.

Published by Pet Chapel® Press (petchapel.com/press). Pet Chaplain® and Pet Chapel® are registered trademarks.

All rights reserved. To use this work for educational purposes, please inquire about licensing opportunities and additional training materials by emailing the authors at: licensing@petchaplain.com. Except as permitted under the United States Copyright Act of 1976, no part of this publication may be reproduced or distributed in any form or by any means, including artificial intelligence systems, or stored in a data base or retrieval system, without prior written permission of the authors, except in the case of brief quotations embodied in critical reviews and certain other noncommercial uses permitted by copyright law.

Book design by Karen Duke.

Paperback ISBN 978-1-969169-04-5
Kindle ISBN 978-1-969169-05-2
Ebook ISBN 978-1-969169-09-0

First edition 2026.

Pet Chaplain® Learning Series

VOLUME 1

Heart Animals
Sacred Stories About Pets Who Change Our Lives

VOLUME 2

Always in My Heart
Coping Creatively with Pet Loss

VOLUME 3

Just an Animal
Reflections on the Human-Animal Bond
and Western Culture

VOLUME 4

Veterinary Chaplaincy
Interfaith Spiritual Care for Pet Loss

Visit petchaplain.com to learn more about the series
and other resources available from Pet Chaplain.

This book is dedicated to our moms,
Helen Gierka and Lois Duke,
who never met an animal or child
they didn't want to love and feed.

How it is that animals
understand things I do not know,
but it is certain that they do understand.
Perhaps there is a language
which is not made of words and
everything in the world understands it.
Perhaps there is a soul hidden
in everything and it can always speak,
without even making a sound,
to another soul.

— Frances Hodgson Burnett, *A Little Princess*

Contents

A Note from the Authors	xiii
Introduction	xix

The Bond

Chapter 1	Our Animal Teachers	3
Discussion Questions: Chapter 1		23

The Loss

Chapter 2	The Hardest Goodbye	27
Chapter 3	Life-Changing, Universe-Shifting Grief	41
Chapter 4	Guilt and Forgiveness	57
Chapter 5	How Culture Shapes Our Grief	69
Discussion Questions: Chapters 2–5		83

Continuing Connection

Chapter 6	Moving On Versus Staying Connected	87
Chapter 7	Coping with Loss	104
Discussion Questions: Chapters 6–7		127

Transformation

Chapter 8	Making Meaning of Loss	131
Chapter 9	Generativity	144
Discussion Questions: Chapters 8–9		153

The Sacred Story Project

Chapter 10　Crafting Your Sacred Story:
　　　　　　Connecting and Coping　　　　　　157

Our Journey Continues　　　　　　169
Acknowledgments　　　　　　170
About the Authors　　　　　　172
Notes　　　　　　173
Selected Bibliography　　　　　　183
Index　　　　　　185

A Note from the Authors

Welcome to the Pet Chaplain Learning Series! I'm Rob Gierka, founder and president of Pet Chaplain, and I'll be your guide for this unique learning experience. In this introductory note, I'll provide some essential information about the series, including an overview of its goals and recommendations for engaging with the books.

This book is the second volume in a four-book set that explores pet keeping and loss in contemporary Western society. If you're passionate about pets, concerned with the well-being of all animals, or simply curious about the human-animal bond, you'll learn a great deal about this remarkable social and cultural phenomenon with this series. If you've recently lost a pet and are struggling with grief—or if you're thinking about a pet lost years before—you'll find the support you need within one or all of the first three books in the series. These volumes examine pet keeping and loss from different angles so you can explore your experience holistically. The fourth book in the series builds on the content of the first three books with a focus on interfaith spiritual care for pet loss, providing an invaluable resource for caregiving professionals and others interested in this new field of spiritual care.

The series addresses four primary questions: Why are our animal companions so important to us? How do we navigate the deep sorrow we experience as we rebuild our lives without their physical presence? How do our social interactions impact our journey of grief when we lose our pets? And how can we best help each other find lasting peace and a renewed sense of purpose? The series explores these queries through a combination of scholarship and storytelling that vividly capture the lived reality of pet keeping and loss in the modern West.

Regarding scholarship, the series takes a broad, interdisciplinary approach. It draws on many academic disciplines, including human-animal studies, clinical psychology, existential psychology, death studies, philosophy, sociology, anthropology, religious studies, history, and neuroscience. This holistic approach is increasingly rare in today's siloed academic world, where most scholars focus solely on their area of expertise. Yet life is not easily divided into neat categories, and I've taken considerable care to synthesize the research cited in the series into a holistic perspective on our complex, continually evolving relationship with the greater-than-human world. Geographically, however, I've had to limit my research because it was impractical to incorporate scholarship for locations outside the West. Most of the research about pet keeping and loss, the human experience of grief, and other topics covered in the series is based on studies conducted in the US and, to a lesser extent, Canada, Australia, and Western Europe.

To balance out all this scholarship, the series includes an abundance of pet stories. These narratives are important not only because people love to read stories but because stories are critical to a good education. There's an old proverb that says: "Tell me the facts, and I'll learn. Tell me the truth, and I'll believe. But tell me a story, and it will live in my heart forever." When you've read everything I have to say about pet keeping and loss, I expect it's the stories you'll remember best.

Many voices make an appearance in the series. I tell my own stories about pets I've loved and lost and the pivotal experiences that have shaped my interest in this new field of spiritual care. You'll read the stories of pet keepers who attended my pet loss support group over the last two decades. You'll gain insight into the veterinary world as I reflect on my service as the on-call chaplain at a large veterinary teaching hospital. You'll read the stories and reflections of people who participated in an online course in veterinary chaplaincy that my co-author Karen Duke and I developed and taught for five years. Finally, you'll discover the amazing insights offered by a small group of aspiring veterinary technologists ("vet techs") who I interviewed for my doctoral research study of the human-animal bond and bereavement.

The four volumes that comprise the series are not textbooks per se, or at least not the kind of textbook you may have read before. As an educational program, the series is modeled on the self-paced courses offered by the Great Books Foundation, a nonprofit organization that promotes lifelong learning through reading and discussion of literature, philosophy, poetry, and other compelling texts. For fourteen years, I participated in a Great Books discussion group with a small group of well-read and highly accomplished octogenarians. It was one of the best learning experiences of my life, and I've long wanted to create a rich, transformative learning experience for others.

One of the series' greatest strengths—and the quality that sets it apart from other books about pet keeping and loss—is its wealth of learning resources. The first three books in the series include thought-provoking questions that encourage critical engagement with many concepts related to pet keeping and loss, giving you the opportunity to articulate your beliefs on a variety of animal-related topics. There are no "right" answers to these questions. Rather, their goal is to promote critical thinking, exploration, analysis, and the clear articulation of your personal perspective on the diverse topics explored in the series. The more time and effort you put into this work, the more you'll learn about yourself and your perspective about animals, death, grief, spirituality, and other topics explored in the series.

You'll also be invited to create what I call a "sacred story"—or, more accurately, a series of stories—about your life as an animal lover, pet keeper, animal advocate, environmentalist, or however you might describe yourself. A sacred story aims to answer some simple but challenging questions: What is your authentic identity as a human being amid all the diverse life-forms on this incredible planet? How have your personal interactions with animals and the natural world shaped your identity? And how can you lead a life in relationship with animals and the natural world that is spiritually directed and in keeping with your values? If such questions are important to you, then you're in the right place.

This kind of contemplative practice is essential in this age of rapid technological, cultural, and environmental change. Amid these vast shifts, many people are adopting new perspectives about the greater-than-human world. The spiritual landscape in the modern West is also changing. Among those who participate in a mainstream faith community, many approach their spiritual lives from a position of searching and questioning. Many people have left mainstream faith communities and are creating spiritual amalgamations that blend scientific understandings of the cosmos with traditional faith traditions and ancient spiritual practices. Still others contemplate the world through a values-based or humanist lens. Wherever you place yourself in this evolving spiritual landscape, the learning series will help you better understand the origins of your values and beliefs about animals and spirituality.

You can read these books from personal interest or to support your healing journey, whether you're anticipating the imminent loss of a pet, actively grieving for a pet, or thinking about a pet lost years ago. The series' learning resources also make it a great fit for book study groups, and I encourage you to seek out others with whom you can share this journey of learning, healing, and spiritual growth. Your group might include your family and friends, coworkers, fellow church members in your place of worship, animal lovers you know through social media groups, or even people you meet at the dog park. Sharing your stories about animals and receiving others' stories with compassion will broaden your perspective on the human-animal bond and expand your ability to appreciate the diverse ways people think about and interact with animals.

The learning series is the culmination of thirty years of study, personal contemplation, spiritual care practice, and creative collaboration with pet keepers, animal advocates, environmentalists, and spiritual seekers. As noted earlier, I'll serve as your narrator and guide throughout the series, but it's important to note that my coauthor Karen has supported me throughout the development process. A talented writer and artist, Karen has helped me condense, organize, and synthesize years of practical insights and scholarship, and she's also contributed her own research to the wealth of scholarship cited in these books. Karen was also the lead writer for the series, so her voice is on every page, even when I appear to be doing all the talking.

Thank you for your interest in the Pet Chaplain Learning Series. Karen and I are delighted and humbled by the opportunity to share all we've learned with you. We hope you enjoy this learning experience and that, wherever your path may take you, you'll have a richer understanding of why animals are such an important part of our lives.

With gratitude—
Rob Gierka, EdD, and Karen Duke

Introduction

When I volunteered as a hospital chaplain in the late 1990s, I had a conversation that defined for me what chaplaincy is all about. It was 2 or 3 a.m., and I was wandering the long, polished hallways of a hospital near my home in Raleigh, North Carolina. I got off the elevator and walked toward the nurse's station near the birthing pods and maternity ward. Three nurses, two women and a man, were chatting at the station, and as I walked by, one of the women called out to me.

"Excuse me. Are you lost?"

Chagrined because I really was lost but didn't want to admit it, I smiled and shrugged. "I'm not lost," I said. "I'm looking for the lost."

"Well, you found him!" the other woman retorted, gesturing at the man.

We all laughed at her joke, but my response to the nurse's question was true. Helping people who feel lost is one important thing that chaplains do. We offer emotional and spiritual support to people who feel adrift, confused, and uncertain, and who are sometimes gripped by despair because of illness, death, and other traumatic events.

In the book *A Grief Observed*, British author C. S. Lewis described the overwhelming sorrow he experienced following the death of his wife, Joy Davidson. "Grief is like a long valley, a winding valley where any bend may reveal a totally new landscape," wrote Lewis.[1]

Many people have told me they felt lost and disoriented after losing a beloved pet. Some said they'd never felt grief that intense. If this has ever happened to you, your days were probably filled with a longing for your animal and a persistent desire to turn back the clock and return to a happier time. Maybe you worried you were going crazy as you struggled to make it through your day without your pet by your side. And maybe you wondered if your pain would ever end.

I wish I could offer an easy solution or a stepwise method for resolving such anguish, but there are no shortcuts through the valley of grief. What I can give you is hope. I've been supporting grieving pet keepers for more than twenty years, and I've seen people bounce back from even the most difficult losses. To give you some inspiration, I'll share the stories of others who've traveled this road and successfully navigated their own grief journeys.

Many pet keepers are surprised at the intensity of their grief, and they worry that perhaps what they're experiencing isn't normal. Pet loss is not well understood in our society, and one of the goals of this book is to explore what grief for a pet looks and feels like. What are the challenges you might face when navigating your pet's end of life? And what are some things you can do to manage your sorrow? Coping with the loss of a pet can be an overwhelming ordeal, especially soon after your animal has died or otherwise been lost. To help you better understand this aspect of your grief journey, we'll explore some practical things you can do to process your feelings and simultaneously honor the animals you've lost. You might be anticipating the loss of a sick pet, mourning for an animal who died recently, reflecting on the loss of a pet who died years ago, or struggling with anger and sadness for all the animals who suffer and die needlessly. No matter your situation, this book will give you a richer understanding of your grief journey.

We often think of grief as an emotional experience, and it is. Yet I believe it's more accurately understood as a spiritual phenomenon, or a creative process through which we learn about ourselves and reconnect with what we hold to be sacred. Human spirituality can be framed in many ways, from the awe and wonder we experience in nature to our sense of connection with a universal force greater than ourselves. Our spirituality can also be understood as our ongoing effort to discover and affirm our authentic identities. The search for meaning and a renewed sense of purpose that we undertake after a loss is a deeply spiritual experience. It is this aspect of human spirituality that this book is concerned with.

One of the greatest challenges we face when we lose a pet concerns our uncertainty about how to manage and express distressing emotions. This phenomenon is, in part, a product of our culture. We live in a grief-avoidant society, and we've been taught to think about grief as something to be cured, as if it were a mental illness. This book offers a different vision of grief, framing it as a wise guide and teacher rather than an archenemy. In the words of chaplain Lisa Irish, "Grieving consciously creates pathways into deeper self-knowledge, invites an increased ability to be grateful, and encourages connections to loved ones that transcend time and space."[2] In other words, our grief can lead us back to what we love. We only need to trust and accept the path we're on and be willing to stay the course.

As the saying goes, tears water our growth. I've personally glimpsed the truth of this bittersweet wisdom and met countless pet keepers whose stories vividly demonstrate its veracity. As you engage with your sorrow and make meaning of your loss, you might learn new things about yourself, tapping into a reservoir of strength you didn't know you had. You might gain insight into the complexity of the human heart, recognizing your unquenchable desire for life and your deep-seated fear of death. You might learn to embrace every moment of your life with greater joy and gratitude. You might also learn something new about your wonderful, fascinating, and complex animal friends, gaining a deeper appreciation for their extraordinary gifts.

Such discoveries are life-altering and soul-shaping. They're the reward for being fully present to all that comes your way. When you have the courage to embrace death and grief as a natural part of life, you might discover a wellspring of gratitude for your blessings and your animal friends. The love you continue to feel for them is like a pilot light—a steady and enduring flame that can ignite your life with meaning and purpose.

I encourage you to be gentle and patient with yourself as you engage with this book and answer the discussion questions that follow each section. These questions will sometimes ask you to call forth memories of loved ones you've lost and carefully examine your feelings, including those that are uncomfortable or painful. Like most people, you've probably had quite a few upsetting experiences you've never thought about and grief you've pushed aside. Many of us are burdened by a tangle of unexamined grief, anger, regret, and guilt. Left to simmer, unexamined feelings often surface in unexpected ways, harming ourselves and others.

Thankfully, of course, life is not all about distressing or painful emotions. While this book explores the grief we experience when we lose a pet, it also celebrates the many gifts we receive from our animal friends. As you read this book, be sure to reflect on the memories of your pet that bring you joy. What do these memories have in common, and why do they make you feel happy? What life-giving lessons did you learn from the important animals in your life? And how have these experiences filled you with love and hope?

If you've recently lost a pet and your grief is intense, you might find it difficult to absorb the information presented here. This is normal and reflects the physiological changes we experience when we're grieving. If you have trouble grasping the ideas offered in these pages, you might want to pick this book up later. You're likely to discover insights down the road that you miss at present.

For readers interested in veterinary chaplaincy, this book is a primer on the human experience of grief. Understanding how people grieve and the social norms that frame how we're expected to grieve in contemporary Western society are essential to your chaplaincy education. This book will also help you process your own losses. Self-awareness is essential for spiritual caregivers because the farther along you are on your own healing journey, the better you'll be able to help others.

Always in My Heart focuses on the personal loss of an animal companion. Yet the journey of grief explored in these pages is traveled by many who work as animal healers, rescuers, and protectors. Veterinary and animal rescue workers regularly suffer moral injury when their jobs require them to do things to animals that they believe are unethical. Many people also grieve the loss of wild animals and the destruction of natural spaces. Like the loss of a pet, such losses are not widely recognized or honored. And because such losses are ongoing and widespread, it can be difficult to sustain your emotional and spiritual equilibrium and your hope for a better future.

If you've ever grieved the loss of a special pet, found yourself moved to tears by stories about unhomed animals being euthanized en masse, felt angered by the rapid extinction of animal species worldwide, or mourned the loss of a champion tree, this book will help you honor your grief and engage with the world with renewed energy and purpose.

The Bond

CHAPTER 1

Our Animal Teachers

There's a passage in the Old Testament that I'm fond of: "But ask the animals, and they will teach thee, or the birds in the sky and they will tell thee, or speak to the earth, and it will teach thee, or let the fish in the sea inform thee" (Job 12: 7–10.) Many Indigenous traditions offer a similar sensibility, recognizing that animals have much to teach us about living in right relationship with others and in balance with nature. In the book *Braiding Sweetgrass*, Native American horticulturalist and author Robin Wall Kimmerer writes, "In Native ways of knowing, human people are often referred to as 'the younger brothers of Creation.' We say that humans have the least experience with how to live and thus the most to learn—we must look to our teachers among the other species for guidance. Their wisdom is apparent in the way that they live. They teach us by example."[1]

I titled this chapter "Our Animal Teachers" because that's the way I think about the creatures with whom we share this planet. Animals may not have opposable thumbs or be able to do complex math, but they possess a lot of love, joy, and simple wisdom.

This chapter is dedicated to the careful contemplation of the powerful life lessons we can learn through the example of our animal companions—our furry, scaled, and feathered teachers—and the amazing gifts we enjoy in their company. Although this book is focused primarily on pet loss and the grief journey we undertake when our companions are no longer with us, I wanted to begin with a focused look at the quality of the human-animal bond at its finest.

To appreciate why losing an animal companion can be so terribly painful, you first must appreciate what has been lost. When you say goodbye to a living creature who loved you no matter what, who was an important part of your daily routines, who was with you through your joys and hardships, who understood you without words ever being spoken, whose warm presence and playfulness filled your days with comfort and joy—well, that's a pretty big loss. Without your animal by your side, your world will never be the same, and the abiding pain you feel when you lose your pet marks this life passage. As you read this chapter, I encourage you to reflect on what you value most about the cat sitting on your lap, doing their best to distract you from this page, or the dog warming your feet.

We'll begin this exploration with an excerpt from my favorite love poem by Elizabeth Barrett Browning: "How do I love thee? Let me count the ways."[2]

Nonjudgmental Love

When asked to identify the one quality they most appreciate about their pets, most people say "unconditional love." In my view, however, the phrase *nonjudgmental love* is more accurate.

Our pets don't judge us. Given a basic level of care, they accept and love us just as we are. They love us on our good days and our bad days. They love us when we're happy or angry, swelling with pride or wallowing in self-pity, greedy for more or grateful for what we have, selfish or generous, and forgiving or harboring a grudge. In contrast, our relationships with other people can be messy. Our friendships and kinships are fraught with misunderstandings, competitiveness, jealousy, anger, controlling behavior, simmering dissatisfaction, and other complexities. We love each other and gain great satisfaction from our authentic connections with other people, but these connections can be harder to maintain than the loving relationships we enjoy with our pets. One of the vet tech students I interviewed, a man named Frank, observed this truth when reflecting on his relationship with his cat, Muppet. "It was a relationship like any other, but in some ways it was better," he said. "Even family members you have arguments with. Even family members you have disagreements with. Yet you love them regardless. Well, that same relationship without those arguments? Without those disappointments? Without those judgments? Without the heartbreak of their disappointments in life? It's pretty easy to maintain that kind of relationship. When you experience unconditional love, you never forget it. And, unfortunately, there are very few humans who can give unconditional love. An animal is born that way."

Pets are often willing to give us the love we need precisely when we need it, and they're also incredibly sensitive and attuned to our moods. An animal's reliable presence does more than simply meet our needs for companionship. Animals can be our refuge in difficult times. A young woman named Kelly had this to say about her childhood pet, a hamster named Daisy: "Daisy was my everything. She was my best friend and my sister and my brother. She was the only thing I really had. I sometimes think, 'Oh, yeah, I had that once.' I had unconditional love from somebody when I really needed it, and I know if I hadn't had that, I probably wouldn't have made it as far as I did in my younger years."

Research into families with pets shows that our pets help us weather difficult times. A study of pets in family settings found that "after a stressful workday, [a pet's] enthusiastic greeting, affection, and nonjudgmental support lead many, on arriving home, to prefer the company of their pets to that of their spouses."[3] When you're going through a tough time—such as a move, divorce, major illness, or the death of a human loved one or another pet—a pet can provide you with much-needed comfort, affection, and a sense of security. These simple gifts may be especially important if you struggle to find adequate support among your family and friends.

The ability of our animals to accept us as we are, without judgment, is powerful. Many people prefer the company of animals to that of people because their relationships with their pets are more consistently rewarding. Animal ethicist James Serpell points to a survey that showed that "nearly half of women . . . said that they relied more on their dogs and cats for affection than on their husbands or children."[4] Another study found that participants sometimes felt closer to their pet than to other family members, particularly if the pet was a dog.[5]

Many adults and children confide in their pets about their troubles. It's easy to understand why kids rely on their pets in this way. Animals don't talk back to the child or correct them when they're wrong. They never tell them not to feel their feelings, as some parents are inclined to do. Their silent, attentive, and gentle presence helps children feel heard, understood, and validated. The stress of talking about their feelings with older siblings or parents—where verbal meanings and nonverbal cues may be mixed—is absent in conversations with pets. In one study, nearly 80 percent of children between the ages of ten and fourteen said that they turned to their pets for comfort when they were upset.[6]

Pets can serve as important role models for people of all ages, teaching us important lessons about love and tolerance. John, a vet tech student, learned a lot about love and reciprocity from his childhood dog Dare. "I had someone I could rely on," John said. "She didn't judge me. She didn't blame me for my clothes being torn or me being all beat up or hearing this other kid was in the hospital because we got into a fight. She loved me no matter what, and I loved her right back. And that's the bond I've had with animals. They don't judge you. They're there for you. They just want to be treated right and loved, and they'll give that love right back."

Forgiveness

Because animals don't judge us, they also tend to be very forgiving. Even animals who've been abused or neglected sometimes rebound with a steady infusion of loving care. Their willingness to quickly forgive those who've hurt them is remarkable. This is not to say that animals don't carry their past hurts with them, because they do. Sadly, as with children who've been abused or neglected, some animals never recover from mistreatment, and the behavioral issues that arise from these experiences, such as aggressiveness and extreme anxiety, make placement in a forever home difficult. But many do recover, and these animals often become loving, devoted companions.

Stories abound of rescued animals who've bounced back from severe neglect and abuse. Many species outside of those traditionally kept as pets appear to possess resilient, forgiving natures. In the book *The Emotional Lives of Animals*, cognitive ethologist Marc Bekoff shares the story of a Chinese moon bear named Jasper. Jasper was confined in what's called a "crush cage," a device that squeezed him into an impossibly tiny space to extract his bile, which is used in traditional Chinese medicine.[7] Although Jasper endured incalculable suffering for fifteen years, he bounced back after being rescued. Described as a "mischievous, fun-loving bear," Jasper befriended every creature and person he met. Bekoff considers Jasper a hero, or the "spokes-bear for hope and freedom," because despite his torture, Jasper forgave.[8]

Notably, forgiveness is central to the teachings of many spiritual traditions. The Buddha advised followers to practice forgiveness to end suffering and bring dignity and harmony to their lives. Similarly, Jesus advised his followers to love and pray for their enemies rather than harbor enmity toward them (Matthew 5:44). Perhaps our animals' ability to forgive the harms done to them and to embrace life with joy can be an inspiration to us.

Authenticity

Animals display their feelings openly and without hesitation. They're like young children in this respect—fully present and emotionally authentic, without the filters and social armor that adults employ to protect themselves. With an animal, what you see is generally what you get. This is not to say that our animal companions don't try to deceive us or other pets in the household. A dog will hide a treat under their paw and wait until another dog has left the room before eating it. Yet most animals aren't very good at deception, because their thoughts and feelings are so apparent.

Such authenticity and trustworthiness are like a breath of fresh air, especially in a world where we interact daily with strangers and it's difficult to reliably know if the people we encounter are being sincere or deceptive. Animals have the innate ability to tap into the innocence and love that we tend to hide and protect in a world that can be competitive, hostile, and unpredictable. Perhaps this is why it's so touching when we see a stereotypical macho man doting on a little dog, cat, or hamster.

In our social lives, most of us are compelled to create different personas for different settings. We might project one persona at work or school, another on social media, another with acquaintances and friends, another with strangers, and yet another in our families. Modern life is stressful in part because we're often expected to switch rapidly between these various roles, like actors on stage.

With our pets, the pressure is off. We don't have to worry about appearances or putting on a good face. We don't have to perform, create a favorable impression, or win anybody over. They give us permission to dispense with the social masks we often wear in our relationships with other people. In the company of our pets, we can be vulnerable and safely reveal our true selves.

Presence

Animals seem to possess an ineffable, immeasurable presence that can warm our hearts, ease our suffering, and open channels of communication that are otherwise closed. This is a powerful gift that helps animals connect with people who struggle to relate with others and the world around them, such as those with autism and Alzheimer's disease. Sigmund Freud, the father of modern psychology, recognized this gift early in his career. When Freud's dog Jofi attended his therapy sessions, he noticed that his patients seemed more comfortable and made greater progress.

An animal's healing presence is a wondrous phenomenon. Jon Katz, a writer who lives on a small Vermont farm, shared a story about his border collie Izzy in the book *Soul of a Dog*.[9] Izzy wasn't much for herding sheep but had a talent for spreading love and happiness. Once Katz discovered Izzy's unique gifts, he began taking him to a local hospice facility. "[Izzy] has a soul I've never encountered in an animal before," Katz wrote. "It comes, I think, from his capacity to see into people, to feel their need, to open deep channels within them. I don't know if he means to, or how he manages it, but I know that he does it. I've seen him do it time and time again, especially among the dying, people living on the edge of life, people who are suffering."[10]

This mysterious *something* Izzy possesses has much to do with his ability to connect deeply and wordlessly with people. Humans are symbolic thinkers, which means we constantly translate our experience into language and ideas. This inclination is at once our strength and our frailty. It's a strength when our facility for conceptual thinking allows us to imagine a world we don't inhabit and create the world we imagine. But it's a frailty because we rarely experience reality directly. Compared to most humans, animals live in a direct, embodied way with ease. They relate to the world with a simplicity that's usually evident only among young children and, sometimes, the aged.

Animals also speak the language of the heart. The language of the heart is felt intuitively and not processed intellectually. It doesn't require spoken or written words, yet it is no less real or valuable than our words. Our animal companions are very good at sensing our moods, and many people feel certain that their pets know exactly how they feel. Many also claim that they can accurately read their animal's emotions—all without words. The eyes are windows to the soul, and our animal friends will look directly into ours with such pure, guileless love that it can be transformative and healing. Kelly, a vet tech student, said she enjoyed a profound connection with her dog Zuzu, a Rottweiler she grew up with. "I remember sitting on the ground as a kid, and she would sit with me," Kelly said. "She would lay her head on my lap and look up at me. I'd talk to her about everything, and she would make me feel so soft and warm and free from everything. I remember knowing that she loved me."

Constancy

For many of us, the rhythm of our daily lives is in sync with that of our pets. Our animals are beside us when we rise in the morning and grab our first cup of coffee. They're beside us when we walk them, stroke them, groom them, play with them, and cuddle with them. There is nothing quite like being greeted by a joyful dog when you arrive home after a stressful day at work and a hellish commute. Even cats are glad to see us when we get home, though they tend to be less effusive than dogs.

Animals are routine-oriented and have amazingly accurate internal clocks. Most will let you know precisely when it's time to get up in the morning, have breakfast, play in the yard, eat a snack, take a nap, take a walk, eat dinner, snuggle up on the couch, and go to bed. Our daily schedules are often built around these routines. Our pets' steady companionship provides an anchor of shared daily routines that buffers us from the frenetic pace of modern life.

Compared to the healing presence discussed earlier, this day-to-day presence seems far less glamorous. Yet such constancy may be just as important, especially for those of us who live alone and rely on our pets for companionship. Even people with jam-packed schedules and lots of social interaction may appreciate a pet's reliable presence. Our pets are never late, and they don't cancel on us. We can count on them to be there, happy to see us, even when we can't count on much else in our lives. That kind of reliability is like pure gold at a time when many of us are struggling to find a secure berth in an increasingly hectic, unpredictable world.

Of course, mundane activities like scooping the kitty litter or cleaning your dog's teeth are not the things we mention when reflecting on our relationships with our pets. But when those activities occur almost every day for years, a sacred trust is created. In sharing the small, intimate details of your lives, you and your pet are telling each other, "I'll be there for you, and you'll be there for me." Studies have found that a pet's loyalty is one of the reasons people feel more secure in their relationships with pets than with human loved ones.[11]

People who've had a pet for a very long time often discover that the longevity of the relationship makes it extraordinary. Frank offered these reflections about his long relationship with his cat Muppet and the routines they shared:

> For twenty-two and a half years, that cat and I bonded. We were friends. We ate together, slept together, did everything together. We had experiences over a lifetime. The relationship was special partly because we were together for so long. . . . We were rarely apart. Every day she'd be there to greet me when I came home from work. Whether my wife was home, my dog was home, it didn't matter who was home—that cat was waiting for me at the door just like a dog. She could tell if it was my car, even if I was blocks away, and, like a dog, she'd sit there waiting. And every day it was a chore to get from the front door to where I was going because she'd do this weaving

thing between my feet. Finally, when I would settle in for the evening, she'd be right there, sitting on my lap while I read or watched TV. She slept with me for years, snuggled behind my knees.

It's a rare gift to share a loving connection with another living being that combines constancy with absolute acceptance. As noted by dog lover and author Caroline Knapp, there is no replacement for "being accompanied through daily life and over the course of years by a creature who bears witness to every change, every shift in mood, everything we do and say and experience, never judging us when we falter or fail."[12]

Touch

One of the things people enjoy most about their pets is petting them. The animals we consider pet-able—or who possess soft fur and appear to enjoy being stroked—are by far the most popular pets. Many people enjoy curling up on the couch with their dog in the evening, lazily stroking their companion's silky coat, or relaxing with a good book and a cat on their lap (or on the book itself). Petting an animal is very pleasurable, and it appears to be equally pleasurable to our animals.

People and furred pets both have sensory neurons called C-tactile afferents on their skin. Stroking stimulates these neurons, triggering the release of oxytocin, a hormone linked to positive feelings, trust, intimacy, social bonding, and wound healing.[13] This sets off a chain reaction of good feelings as levels of stress hormones drop, blood pressure decreases, and heart rates slow. Touching also releases endorphins that increase good feelings and decrease pain. Affection itself has a unique chemical signature. Studies have shown that pet keepers with high oxytocin levels and low levels of the stress-related hormone cortisol reported stronger emotional bonds with their animals.[14]

It's no wonder that animals make such great partners in human health-care settings. Because of their calming influence, animals are used to treat conditions that are caused or exacerbated by stress, including hypertension and conditions that carry high levels of anxiety, such as Alzheimer's disease and autism. Many people are touch-deprived. Americans, in particular, tend to have a very strong sense of personal space, like an invisible force field that wards off intruders. Physical contact between strangers or casual acquaintances is frowned upon. People who live alone may be especially touch deprived. Similarly, children may not experience physical affection in their families, and their interactions with adults, such as teachers, may lack physical contact because of fears about inappropriate touching.

Generally, this prohibition doesn't apply to animals. We can hug, stroke, and roll around on the floor with our animals to our hearts' desire without raising an eyebrow. My grand-dog Millie, an energetic border collie-poodle mix, *needs* to be touched. She's an athletic dog who is as graceful as a gazelle when she bounds around the backyard or at the dog park. With her long legs and slender body, she doesn't fit comfortably on my lap, but that's where she wants to be whenever she can manage it. During my frequent visits, she and I enjoy a morning routine in which she positions herself between my legs. I squeeze my legs and wrap her in my arms, giving her a full-body hug. I think we both enjoy a wonderful sense of connection with those great big hugs, and I can't think of a better way to say, "Good morning! I'm so glad to see you!"

Psychologists who study the quality of attachment between people and their pets assert that physical contact with our animals is an important aspect of the human-animal bond. According to *attachment theory*, one of the most important aspects of our relationships with others—whether with people or pets—is known as "safe haven," and safe haven is grounded in physical contact.[15] Humans and other highly social mammals develop a sense of safe haven as infants through close physical contact with their primary caregivers. A study of disabled people with service animals found that a "key feature of the safe haven component was contact comfort, paralleling the cuddling, prolonged skin-to-skin contact and mutual gazing that characterizes infant-caregiver and romantic relationships."[16]

Many pet keepers have discovered the healing power of physical contact with an animal and have become involved in alternative healing modalities that are grounded in touch, such as massage or Reiki. Reiki is an energy healing technique in which practitioners use their hands to improve the flow and balance of energy in the body. Cindi Rodriguez, a graduate of my veterinary chaplaincy course, became a Reiki practitioner after her dog Mercedes began showing weakness in her hind legs and aggression toward other dogs. Rather than medicate her, Cindi chose the path of touch therapy. What surprised her was how much she personally benefited from her massage and Reiki work with Mercedes. "The power of touch provided Mercedes with more benefits than I expected," Cindi said. "In addition to significantly calming her anxieties and giving her relief from her arthritic pain and discomfort, the heart and soul connection that we shared became even deeper."

Living in the Moment

One of the things we value most about our pets is their ability to enjoy each moment. This would appear to be a simple thing, but it's remarkably difficult for humans to be fully present in the here and now because we obsess so much about the past and the future. We perceive the passage of time differently from our animal companions, and, though I cannot say with certainty why this is the case, it's an interesting phenomenon.

It strikes me that the human mind is like a cineplex, or a movie theater with three enormous screens arranged side by side. Different films are playing on all three screens simultaneously. On the left screen, footage of our memories constantly unwinds as we spin endless stories about ourselves and our experiences. In the center screen lies the present moment, and on the right screen is the future, where we project our hopes and fears. The images, thoughts, and sensations we project on our past and future screens can range from a few minutes to many years in the past or future. One moment you might be worrying about your current dog who isn't feeling well, and in the next moment your thoughts switch to a dog you lost thirty years ago. We also construct alternate realities in our minds, imagining the future and things that don't yet exist. Psychological researchers refer to the phenomenon of switching seamlessly from past to present to future as "mental time travel."[17]

Many animals appear to share this three-screen cineplex. Recent scientific understandings of animal cognition show that many species have a screen for the past. They have memories, appear to learn from their experiences, and will pursue courses of action that reflect this learning. This includes proactively avoiding situations and people that have previously caused them discomfort or pain. Animals also appear to think about the future. Many species of wild animals, such as wolves, coordinate their actions to pursue future goals, for example, by hunting prey or seeking safety. Similarly, many pets anticipate our arrival at the end of our workdays with remarkable accuracy and are ready and waiting to storm the front door when it opens.

This is not to say that animals revisit their past with great anxiety or fret about the future in quite the same way as humans. Our ability to reflect critically on past experiences and modify our actions based on those experiences is a powerful way of being in the world. We can imagine the future we want to create and manipulate our environment to bring it into being. From an evolutionary perspective, our three-screen cineplex and our ability to flip instantly from the past to the future have helped us adapt to the world in amazing ways.

Yet this skill comes at a considerable cost. We often project our past hardships and fears onto the present and future, even though we cannot predict that the future will be like the past. Many of us are inclined to anticipate the worst outcomes and grow anxious. Unlike our animal friends, we must work very hard to stay focused on the present. Buddhist monks spend their entire lives training their minds to focus on the center screen (the present moment) of their internal cineplex. When they're able to do so, it's believed they reach nirvana—a perfect state of transcendent happiness. Many pet keepers would consider the experience of being with their animal to be a taste of nirvana. Animals have much to teach us about the beauty of living in the moment and embracing life with joy. Many of us would probably be a lot happier if, like our animal friends, we could relax and enjoy the present moment rather than dwelling on the past and future.

Joy and Play

Studies have shown that one of the top reasons people keep pets is that they're fun to watch and have around.[18] Their presence can make our most mundane tasks a little lighter and our moments of joy richer and more memorable. If we've had a stressful day and need a good belly laugh, a strong dose of dog kisses or cat purrs can do the trick, though a funny cat video will do in a pinch. Best of all, an animal's joyfulness and love of play can be infectious.

Many people consider their animal companions their best friends or sidekicks, and an increasing number of dog lovers are bringing their favorite pooches on outdoor adventures, including hiking, running, rock climbing, snow skiing, and boating. In keeping with this trend, it's now possible to purchase durable dog harnesses, GPS trackers, travel water bottles and bowls, first-aid kits, paw protection (boots and balm), pet apparel for different weather (jackets and cooling vests), and specialized gear like doggy backpacks, life jackets, and even dog-friendly tents.

Like adults, children benefit from their playful interactions with pets. For those who lack regular contact with parents and siblings, pets can be a vital presence. As noted by scholar Gail Melson in the book *Why the Wild Things Are*, "For many children in contemporary

America, pets are more likely to be part of growing up than are siblings or fathers. The percentage of children likely to be living with one or more pets sometime between birth and adulthood is estimated to be as high as 90 percent."[19] Moreover, an estimated 75 percent of US children live with pets—a higher proportion than those who live with both parents.[20]

Children often refer to their pets as their brothers or sisters. Their friendships are grounded in shared adventures, favorite activities, and camaraderie. Colleen, one of the vet tech students I interviewed, enjoyed reminiscing about her childhood dog, a dachshund named Pretzel. The two went everywhere together. Summer weekends were spent fishing and mushroom hunting, and she also liked to perch Pretzel on her bicycle handlebars. "I would pick him up, put him on the handlebars, and hold his little feet," Colleen recalled. "We'd ride around the neighborhood, and everyone would laugh because he was so cute. He loved it. . . . I never had a little brother or sister to play with, so Pretzel was all I had. That's why I used to dress him up in baby doll clothes and paint his nails. He was like my little brother."

Another student, Rachel, spent a lot of time with her dog Raffi while her parents were at work. "It was just the two of us in our own world, and everybody else didn't really exist," Rachel said. "When you're playing and having fun as a child and you have a pet who will let you put hats on him and do silly things and not try to move away from you—it was so much fun. I didn't have someone judging me or telling me, 'You're acting crazy,' or 'Hats don't belong on dogs.' For me, those things were just pure, innocent fun."

As noted earlier, John's dog Dare helped him cope with a difficult childhood. When he was a kid, he was often unhappy and angry, and he got into many fights at school. Dare, who John described as "really energetic and always happy," lifted his spirits. "I'd come home from another bad day at school, and Dare would be sitting on the front step," John recalled. "I'd sit down with her, and she'd put her nose in my lap and nudge my hand, flip it up, and get me to pet her. She'd roll over on her back and let me pet her belly. She loved that. I'd start petting her, and it seemed like whatever was going on just wasn't that bad. Just the way she'd look and tilt her head to the side, and those eyes would reflect how I was feeling, it always took the edge off my mood. She knew I was hurting, but petting her and walking her would help me out. I'd pet her until a lot of the pain subsided. Then I'd play ball with her. That helped get that bad energy out of me."

It's almost impossible to feel stressed or unhappy when you spend time with an animal who is consistently happy and full of playful energy. When you're in their company, you can return to the innocent joy and wonder that's the best part of childhood.

Someone to Love

Many of us treat our pets much as we would a favored child. Maybe you're one of these nurturing souls: the woman with a tabby tucked away in a pink baby stroller; the doting business tycoon who leaves his entire multimillion-dollar fortune to his cocker spaniel; or the young couple that celebrates their dog's birthday with presents and a doggie cake. The proportion of people who regard their pet as a child has been rising in recent decades. In 2001, 83 percent of American pet keepers referred to themselves as their animal's "mommy" or "daddy," compared to only 55 percent as recently as 1995.[21] By 2015, referring to a pet as a child had become so common that the phrase *fur baby* was added to the *Oxford English Dictionary*.[22]

Pets are a lot like children, so they meet a very real need for people who enjoy nurturing others. Humans are biologically wired to care for the very young and vulnerable, whether human or animal. Studies have shown that when you give someone a puppy or kitten, they often respond as they do to a human infant, stroking and cuddling the young animal while cooing and speaking softly.[23] Any sign of distress is met with immediate attempts to soothe and comfort the animal. A neurological study of women, their babies, and their dogs showed that "as far as our brains are concerned, dogs and children are equally lovable. . . . The bond between humans and dogs tugs at the same heartstrings—or at least stimulates the same brain centers—as the bond between a mother and her child."[24]

Pets are like toddlers who never grow up. Their innocence and absolute trust in their caregivers are never tainted by the cynicism and rebellion that naturally arise in human children as they mature and become more independent. Consequently, the emotional attachment pet parents feel for their animals can be profound. For some, their pet gives them a reason to get up in the morning, and caring for their pet provides a much-needed sense of meaning and purpose.

For people who see themselves as pet parents, attending to their animal's needs is one of their greatest pleasures. Frank was one of those doting pet parents. He took great pride in the fact that, under his care, his cat Muppet lived for nearly twenty-three years, which is significantly longer than the average lifespan for a domestic cat and is especially impressive because Muppet was the runt of the litter. "I took care of her, from feeding her with an eyedropper to the time she passed away," Frank said. "I made an effort to make sure she had the best food, appropriate exercise, and regular vaccinations."

Pet parenting is particularly popular among millennials. In one study, more than three-quarters of millennials (born between 1981 and 1996) kept pets, and among them, 82 percent considered their pets "starter children."[25] Many said their desire to practice parenthood contributed to or was the main reason for getting an animal. Young adults also tend to spend lavishly on their pets, purchasing the best quality food and luxury items such as beds, toys, clothing, travel accessories, gifts, and grooming services. I've met millennial pet keepers who give their pets an allowance, house their pets in their own bedrooms, sing lullabies to them at bedtime and bath time, celebrate their pets' birthdays with the same enthusiasm as they would a human child, and keep multiple animals to ensure their pets have company.

Among baby boomers, pet keeping has always been popular, and the baby boom generation has been a driving force in its growth since the 1970s. Many are either retired or nearing retirement, so they have more time and energy to devote to their pets than when they were younger. Senior citizens who keep pets often form strong emotional bonds with their animals, especially if they live alone. As noted by one woman who'd lost her spouse, siblings, and only child, her birds are "more precious than you can imagine. They are all I have left in this world."[26] For elderly people who are isolated and cut off from their grown children or other family members, a pet may be their sole source of loving contact with another living creature. In addition, because our society tends to value youth over age and wisdom, caring for their pet provides a tangible way for older people to feel needed and valued. The daily tasks associated with keeping a pet, such as feeding, playing, grooming, and exercising, can lend much-needed structure to long days that may lack meaningful direction or purpose. In this way, a pet can truly be a lifeline for older adults.

While nurturing and loving an animal comes naturally to some people, the pendulum of love swings the other way. We love our pets in part because they return our love so well. While it's true that we sometimes rescue our pets—saving them from an uncertain future in a rescue, shelter, or a life on the streets—it's also true that our animal friends sometimes save us. A woman's reflections about her cat speak to this experience. The woman had adopted an obese cat from a shelter, and she worked hard to bring the cat's weight down to a healthy level. "People say I saved you as you gradually lost weight and could finally walk well, climb the stairs, reach to scratch your ear, and groom yourself," she wrote. "However, I know you really saved me. You gave me so much more, comforting me in times of need and loving me. You taught me the importance of loving and comforting others, taking care of oneself, exploring new things, persevering despite adversity, and enjoying each day."[27]

. . .

In this chapter, we've explored the joys of pet keeping and the unique gifts our animal companions bring to our lives. Their loving spirits, joyful personalities, reliable presence, ability to live fully in the moment, and many other fine qualities enrich our lives. They keep us grounded and offer life-sustaining moments of joy and loving connection. If you keep pets, I expect you can relate to many of these observations and probably add to them.

Perhaps my portrayal of the animals we hold close to our hearts idealizes them and seems unrealistic. It's important to acknowledge that, like us, our animal friends have their foibles. Many share our frailties and challenges. They know jealousy and anger, sorrow and grief. They can be anxious and sometimes don't get along with other animals and some people. But while our pets are not perfect, there is much to celebrate about them. I believe we need to be conscientious about acknowledging their unique gifts while also considering how we might strive to live up to their example.

Given the remarkable rewards our animal companions bring to our lives, it's no wonder so many of us experience intense and long-lasting grief when we lose them. I encourage you to keep the qualities described here fresh in your mind as we engage in a frank discussion of death and grief in the coming chapters. As you'll see, it is the love we continue to feel for our lost pets that sustains us after we lose them, and it is this abiding love that can transform our sorrow into a deep, focused sense of meaning and purpose.

CHAPTER 1

Discussion Questions

1. This chapter describes nine qualities that our animal companions bring to our lives. Select three that were apparent in an animal you've known. Describe the specific ways this animal exhibited these qualities and how your interactions with them felt to you.

2. Of the qualities described in this chapter, which ones are most important to you and why?

The Loss

CHAPTER 2

The Hardest Goodbye

One chilly November morning when I was about sixteen, my mom discovered two newborn kittens in our basement. The mother cat was nowhere to be found. We weren't sure how she got in and out of the basement, and we weren't sure if she would show up again to care for her small litter, so we felt we had no choice but to care for the kittens ourselves.

One of the kittens was a good-sized fellow with black-and-gray stripes. We named him Oscar. We used one of my sister's baby doll bottles to feed him some milk, and he ate well. The second kitten was a tiny orange tabby I named Peanut because she looked just like a peanut when she curled up in my hand. Feeding Peanut was nothing like tending to her ravenous brother. I remember holding her tiny body in the crook of my arm and gently coaxing her to take a little milk from a finger cot I'd put on the end of my pinky. Every morning before school, every afternoon when I got home, and before I went to bed, I tried to get Peanut to eat. When she managed to drink a little milk or eat a bit of food, or when she curled up on my lap for a nap, purring softly, my heart swelled, and I felt sure that better days were ahead.

But despite my efforts, Peanut stayed small and scrawny and spent her days curled up at the base of the refrigerator where warm air blew out of the vent. Then one day, I noticed that she had begun to wheeze. I could hear her breath whistling in and out, and her little round belly rose and fell with the effort. My mom decided we should take her to the veterinarian to see if anything could be done to help her. We didn't have much money, so a trip to the veterinarian was a big deal.

After a gentle examination, the doctor said Peanut had pneumonia and that we should either put her down or give her a shot of penicillin. I was pleased when my mother chose the penicillin, and I felt certain that Peanut would recover. But on the way home from the clinic, Peanut became restless. She kept trying to climb up the front of my mom's blouse, and my mom had to hold her tight. By the time we arrived home, Peanut had died in my mom's arms.

We tearfully wrapped Peanut's tiny body in a small towel, placed her in a shoe box, and buried her in the backyard next to other animals we'd lost. My mom, my younger siblings, and I held hands and said a few words in honor of her short life. Although we didn't have Peanut for long, I felt sad that she didn't thrive. I didn't regret choosing the penicillin shot rather than euthanasia, and I hoped she hadn't suffered too much in the end. But I also remember thinking that there must have been something more we could have done to keep her alive. In hindsight, I think the hardest part of losing Peanut was the feeling of helplessness when I couldn't save her.

In this chapter, we'll begin our exploration of the long, winding valley of grief with a discussion of the many ways we lose our pets. Sometimes the loss begins well before an animal passes away, such as when their health gradually declines, and you're faced with a series of difficult treatment decisions. You might wonder if you're euthanizing at the right time. You might struggle to say goodbye because you can't be certain of your animal's wishes or how they're feeling. Death can also arrive unexpectedly, with no forewarning, leaving you reeling with shock and disbelief. Pets are also lost in ways that don't involve their death, such as when an animal runs away or must be relinquished, yet they are lost to you all the same.

No matter how a pet is lost, what is common to these scenarios is our great discomfort with helplessness. Knowing that sometimes there's nothing we can do to save our animals weighs heavily on our hearts and is one of the most difficult aspects of the grief journey. The goal of this chapter is to encourage you to reflect on your own losses. If you've recently lost a pet, it can be helpful to describe every detail of the experience. People who attend my pet loss support group sometimes review the circumstances of their pet's death or loss multiple times. As painful as this can be, describing your loss can help you gain clarity on what transpired and make sense of a confusing series of events.

Anticipating the Loss

If a pet manages to avoid accidents and major illnesses, their health typically declines slowly, and the signs of their decline can be subtle and easy to overlook. Perhaps your dog is unwilling to walk as far as they used to, or your cat naps longer than usual in that sunny patch by the dining room window. Maybe your animal has begun to eat a little less and is slowly losing weight, until one day you notice the outlines of their bones beneath their fur. You might feel a vague sense of dread tugging at your heart, making it difficult to enjoy carefree moments with your animal.

These are the signs of *anticipatory grief*, a term coined by psychiatrist Erich Lindemann in 1944 and generally defined as grief experienced before a death or loss occurs.[1] Anticipatory grief presents a precarious balancing act between the certainty that death will come someday and your equal certainty that you can't imagine life without your pet. Navigating a pet's end of life can be economically, physically, and emotionally taxing. You might struggle with high veterinary bills and walk around in a fog because you're exhausted from getting up multiple times every night to dispense medication or comfort your animal. You might be overwhelmed with worry about how the end will finally come, if your pet will suffer, and whether you'll be able to cope with your pet's death when it finally arrives. You might feel resentful toward people whose pets are still young and healthy and find yourself avoiding places where healthy animals are present, such as your local dog park or the routes where you used to walk with your dog. You might also feel isolated from your family and friends as you devote all your time and energy to caring for your pet.

You can try to prepare yourself emotionally for your impending loss but still be shocked by how much it hurts when your animal's life comes to an end. A young man named Bryan, who I met in my pet loss support group, shared a story about his dog, Ringo, that speaks to this challenge. Bryan had kept many animals in his life and was familiar with the grief that accompanies their loss. He and his wife had done a lot of research about children and pet loss to better prepare their young daughter for the day when Ringo would no longer be with them. Their daughter adjusted pretty well to Ringo's absence. But Brian and Gwen did not. Despite all their careful preparations, Bryan and Gwen were surprised by how much it hurt when Ringo passed and how intensely they missed having him around.

"We were just in shock," Bryan told me. "I was surprised at how upset I was, and I was surprised at how upset my wife was. She's experienced a lot of death with people who were close to her. As a natural survival mechanism, I think she'd learned how to compartmentalize her feelings. I guess I just didn't think it would hit her that hard. But she was very upset, and I was very upset."

Deciding When to Euthanize

The word *euthanasia* is Greek for "good death." Yet from the perspective of someone who decides to purposely end the life of an animal they love, it can be difficult to see the good in it. Even when you acknowledge that euthanasia is a humane choice for ending an animal's suffering, it's still an agonizing decision. Beyond the moral challenge this common practice presents, it's difficult to decide when it's time to take the final walk with your pet.

I've heard it said that there is no perfect time to euthanize an animal. Euthanize too soon, and you'll rob your pet of more life; wait too long, and your pet will suffer needlessly. The goal is to time the euthanasia at the point when your animal is no longer able to function but before they're in severe and unmanageable pain. This decision hinges on an often murky and subjective judgment call about your animal's quality of life.

When assessing an animal's quality of life, veterinarians don't follow a standard protocol, so the guidance they offer varies. Many factors are considered, including the animal's pain level (which can be difficult to judge because animals often don't show pain); their ability to breathe normally or without oxygen; a significant change in appetite such that hand feeding or a feeding tube is required; hydration level; hygiene, or whether an animal can control their evacuation or evacuate without assistance; mobility, or the animal's ability to move about on their own; happiness, or whether the animal is able to enjoy favorite activities; and an overall more-good-days-than-bad-days evaluation that considers all these factors. Many online tools for evaluating an animal's quality of life are now available, but they're complex and require constant monitoring and daily judgment calls.

This evaluation process can be frustrating and stressful. You want what's best for your animal, but it can sometimes be hard to clearly understand their condition. Monitoring your pet to assess their quality of life can easily become an anxious obsession, as you watch your animal's every move, worrying that a refused meal or an extended nap is the beginning of the end. Your veterinarian can help you with this evaluation, but legally only you can decide to euthanize your animal. You also know your pet best, and you're the only one who can judge your ability to care for them. Ultimately, the choice falls to you and, in the case of a family pet, you and your family members.

The decision about when to euthanize can also be complicated by advances in medical technology. Deciding on treatment versus euthanasia is not always straightforward. Illnesses and injuries that used to result in death are now treatable, but you also might face complex decisions in which your animal's well-being, your moral well-being, and your pocketbook are on the line. Veterinarians are keenly aware of this emerging dilemma. In an interview for the American Veterinary Medical Association, Dr. Steven Marks, former associate dean and director of veterinary services at the North Carolina State University's veterinary teaching hospital, remarked on the ethical dilemmas that are arising in veterinary clinics with greater frequency in recent years. "A decade ago in veterinary medicine, you could say, 'This is a ten-year-old dog, and it will cost $5,000 to treat it,'" Marks said. "And that would've been a deterrent for a lot of pet owners. . . . That's not the case anymore. Now, a ten-year-old dog is treated like a five-year-old dog, and money is not always a restriction for certain clients. Yet is it always in the interest of an animal patient to prolong its life? The question. . .was being asked more and more at the teaching hospital, by staff, faculty, and students."[2]

Euthanizing a pet often entails ethical and emotional struggle. Perhaps you hope your animal will pass peacefully on their own, freeing you from the need to make that dreaded phone call to your veterinarian. You might be flooded with regret, wishing you'd spent more time with your pet, and you might pursue additional treatments to buy yourself more time. If you've been caring for your pet for a long time, you may feel worn out by the constant demands of caregiving. When your animal is euthanized, you might feel relieved that you will no longer need to devote so much time, energy, and money to caring for your animal, and then feel guilty for feeling relieved. You might also feel guilty for choosing to end your animal's life, even when you believe it's the humane thing to do. Studies have shown that pet keepers who euthanize a pet suffer more intense grief and, in particular, long-lasting feelings of guilt compared to people whose pets died naturally of disease or old age or were killed in an accident.[3]

The challenge of timing a euthanasia is exacerbated by the fact that we can't ask our animals what they want or how they're feeling, whether they want to go through another round of painful treatments to extend their life, or if they're ready to die. We rarely face such uncertainty when a human loved one is dying. In cases where someone's wishes are unknown and they're either unconscious or are otherwise unable to make their wishes clear, we're legally prohibited in most US states from purposely delivering death to people as we do with animals.

Despite such challenges, many pet keepers have told me it was their pet who decided when they were ready to go. They can't say the words, but their eyes speak volumes—a phenomenon sometimes described as "eye talk." My friend and chaplaincy colleague Fran Prem recalled the moment when she knew it was time to say goodbye to her "Zen dog" Raffi. "While still fully present, Raffi had become progressively less mobile and was experiencing increasing pain," Fran said. "One morning, he was crossing the driveway and stopped, looked hopeless, and just lay down on the gravel. This is something he would never do normally. When I went to him, he just looked at me and asked for it to stop."

Even when you're certain your animal is in pain and euthanasia is the most loving thing you can do, ending the life of your pet is still painful. Watching your animal suffer is heartbreaking, and ending your animal's life is also heartbreaking. A man I know made the tough decision to euthanize his dog who had terminal cancer. Although he was certain it was the right thing to do, he still felt like he'd betrayed his best friend. Though it had been five years since his dog passed, this man still felt deeply conflicted about his decision. "My wife and I decided it wasn't fair to him to be going downhill like he was and suffering like he was," he said. "So we decided that I would take him to get euthanized. And I did. It was the most horrible thing I have ever had to do, and I still feel guilty about it every day. I know it was for the best, but it was just horrible. On our last day, I came home from work early. He and I went and got two cheeseburgers. We came home, and he ate them. We went for a walk. We came back to the house and sat down. He lay his head in my lap and took a nap. And then I had to take him and have him put down. That's terrible. I think about it every day."

People who make peace with the decision to euthanize generally describe it as placing their pet's right to a comfortable existence free of pain ahead of their need to keep their pet alive. Thinking of euthanasia as a final act of love may help lessen the sting of the decision. Lillian, a vet tech student, described the long and difficult process she went through before finally deciding to euthanize her cat, Freddie. After much heartache and worry, she finally concluded that ending his suffering was the most compassionate, loving thing she could do. "Any kind of treatment was only prolonging and quite possibly putting him in more pain, and I didn't want that," she said. "For sixteen years, Freddie had given me unconditional love. He'd given me so much, and he deserved unconditional love back. He deserved that gift."

Final Words

In the book *Dying Well: Peace and Possibilities at the End of Life*, Dr. Ira Byock describes three things we should say to a loved one who is nearing death and with whom we are on good terms: I love you. I forgive you. Do you forgive me?[4]

When a human loved one is approaching death, exchanging these words can be a precious gift that helps us make peace with our past mistakes and say goodbye to our loved one with a clear conscience. Yet we have little certainty about our animals' inner thoughts and feelings. You might worry that your animal doesn't fully appreciate how deeply they are loved, or you might think your animal blames you for whatever pain they've suffered or for ending their life too soon.

You might also feel desperate to gain access to your animal's inner world and to know, with the precision and certainty of words, that they forgive you, love you, and are at peace. This uncertainty might trouble you long after your animal is gone.

A man who'd lost his long-time companion, a dog named Bella, commented eloquently on this dilemma. A therapist by profession, the man was frustrated by his inability to have a conversation with Bella before her death. "I think the hardest thing about Bella's death was the fact that she couldn't talk," he said. "I talked to her, but she couldn't talk back. When a person dies, you have some words to go by, things that you shared. You have memories of them talking, saying something to you. But with a dog, it's different. It's all moments, just feelings. There were no words. She didn't talk. I saw Bella's face when she died. They pushed in the drug, and within ten seconds, she was dead. It was just so sudden, so overwhelming, and so sad."

Although you can't be certain that your animal understands you, this doesn't mean you should stifle your final words of love and gratitude. It's important to talk with your pet in their final moments, saying the words you need to say. They probably understand far more than you think, and they certainly can hear the love in your voice. Voicing your feelings of love and gratitude opens a spiritual space in those precious final moments with your pet. It also gives you the opportunity to take an important step toward making meaning of your pet's death.

When Death Is Sudden

Watching your pet's gradual decline due to old age or a chronic illness is agonizing. It's equally agonizing to end your animal's life with euthanasia and wonder what they're thinking and feeling. Yet in these situations, you can generally anticipate and recognize the contours of the road you're traveling. But when a pet is lost suddenly due to an accident or a fast-moving illness, it can be like getting hit from behind. Time stops. Nothing feels real. The world keeps turning. The people around you seem to carry on as if nothing has happened, but your life has changed completely in an instant.

These situations—knowing your pet is going to die or being blindsided by sudden loss—are painful in different ways. As psychologist and author Therese Rando writes, "In both sudden death and anticipated death, there is pain. However, while the grief is not greater in sudden death, the capacity to cope is diminished. Grievers are shocked and stunned by the sudden loss of their loved one."[5]

I've heard countless stories about animals who died because of accidents that couldn't be anticipated or prevented. I've also heard stories about animals who died from illnesses that progressed so quickly that nothing could be done to save their lives. The experience of my coauthor Karen with her dog Sarah speaks to this challenge. An energetic border collie, Sarah was a headstrong dog who loved to chase Frisbees. At thirteen, she had begun to slow down, but she was still an enthusiastic play buddy. Then one day, Karen noticed that Sarah wasn't jumping for the Frisbee like she usually did and discovered that one of Sarah's ankles was swollen. Karen was concerned but not alarmed, thinking maybe Sarah had twisted it. Like most animals, Sarah was remarkably stoic. She'd been known to run headlong into a fence and act like the collision was nothing at all.

But then Sarah's health suddenly took a turn for the worse. Overnight, her belly became swollen, and she couldn't walk. A week after the swelling in her ankle first appeared, tests revealed tumors throughout Sarah's body, and the veterinarian said she was in a lot of pain. At thirteen, she probably wouldn't survive a lengthy and difficult treatment regimen. Euthanasia seemed to be the only choice.

Karen was shocked. What caused the cancer? How did it progress so quickly? Were there signs she had missed? Karen was angry with herself and felt guilty for not being more attentive to Sarah. She still sometimes wonders what might have happened if she'd taken Sarah to the veterinarian when she first noticed the swelling in her ankle.

We seek answers to such "what if" questions, but we can't turn back the clock. Like grief, death arrives on its own terms. Sometimes it creeps into our lives gradually, perhaps even in an orderly fashion, and sometimes it appears in a blinding instant. Both experiences are suffused with uncertainty, helplessness, and the unavoidable knowledge that your life will never be the same.

Gone But Not Gone

When a pet is lost and their fate is unknown, the grief that we experience is referred to as *ambiguous*. The term was coined by psychologist Pauline Boss in the book *Ambiguous Loss: Learning to Live with Unresolved Grief*. "Of all the losses experienced in personal relationships," Boss wrote, "ambiguous loss is the most devastating because it remains unclear, indeterminate."[6]

Ambiguous losses occur in various ways in the pet-keeping world. I've encountered many people whose pets were euthanized or rehomed by their families without discussion. Some were assured that their pet was "in a better place" or happily living elsewhere. Many people also have painful memories of watching their parents abandon a pet. Hospice chaplain Shirley Martka, who studied with me in my veterinary chaplaincy course, shared the story of how her father dropped off their family dog by the side of the road as they were moving to a different town. Shirley, who was seven years old at the time, was shocked, as were her three older brothers. They all yelled at their dad to stop the car, but he kept driving, insisting that dogs weren't allowed in their new home.

Shirley kept the sorrow of that terrible memory locked in her heart for sixty years. She'd never shared her story with anyone outside her family until she wrote about it while participating in the course. "I've never shared or spoken to anyone else because of the hurt and the embarrassment with my dad, as a preacher, that he could do something so heartless," Shirley wrote. "I am seventy years old, and when my brother and I speak of our dog, we see him running behind our car, and my brother and I still cry and have to stop talking about it. As much as we loved our dog, our dad just drove away and left our dog as though he were nothing. I don't believe we've ever forgiven my father."

I've heard many stories like this, and my heart breaks for the children who experienced them. Some people are haunted for years by worries about their lost pets, and they feel angry and betrayed by their parents—feelings that are often never talked about or acknowledged. Some also feel guilty for abandoning their pet, even though, as children, they had little to no agency in the situation.

Ambiguous losses also occur when a pet disappears, gets lost, runs away, develops an illness, or takes a medication that drastically alters their personality, behavior, and physical abilities. Animals who suffer from dementia typically change gradually over time, and as the disease progresses, it can seem that the pet they once were has been replaced by a strange animal who bears no resemblance to their former self. You still have your pet physically, but otherwise, they're already gone.

Another circumstance associated with ambiguous loss is when you're forced to relinquish your pet against your wishes. You might have suffered an unexpected illness or injury or lost your job or home. Moving is another common reason for pet relinquishment, and sometimes an individual or family is forced to move to an apartment or home where pets are not allowed because affordable options are impossible to find. In addition, some animals have significant behavioral issues, such as dangerous aggression in dogs, and may need to be rehomed (and sometimes euthanized) after attacking and injuring another animal or a person.

People with a registered service animal, such as a guide dog, must relinquish their animal when they reach mandatory retirement age, typically after eight years of service or when the dog is about ten years old. At that point, the individual will typically adopt a younger service animal. Some people try to adopt their retired service animal as a pet, but this may not be possible in institutional settings where pets (as opposed to service animals) are prohibited. Although retired service animals often go to loving homes, being forced to relinquish an animal you've depended on for years and whom you love deeply is heartbreaking.

No matter what the circumstances of an ambiguous loss, the grief you experience is likely to be defined by confusion and ambivalence. Your pet is neither with you nor are they fully and completely gone as they would be if they had died. You might experience an unnerving, contradictory sense of presence and absence. It's like riding a roller coaster as you rise and fall between hope and hopelessness. Pauline Boss characterizes this experience as one of emotional ambivalence. "Because of the ambiguity," she writes, "loved ones can't make sense out of their situation and emotionally are pulled in opposing directions—love and hate for the same [loved one]; acceptance and rejection of their caregiving role; affirmation and denial of their loss."[7]

If you've suffered an ambiguous loss, you might wonder: Is my pet alive or dead? Who is taking care of them? Do they miss me? Are they angry with me because I wasn't there for them? When you don't know what has happened to your pet—whether your animal is alive or dead, cared for or abandoned—you might imagine all kinds of distressful outcomes. One of the students I interviewed, a young woman named Rachel, described the emotional struggles she went through when she lost her dog, Raffi. When Rachel was nine years old, her parents left Raffi behind when they relocated for work. At first, a family friend cared for Raffi, but Rachel later learned that the friend had given Raffi away. Uncertain about his fate, Rachel agonized for years about where Raffi might be and what his life was like. "Once I found out that Raffi wasn't with my dad's friend anymore, I was worried," Rachel said. "I remember thinking, Where is he now? I never knew what happened to him after that. . . . I still feel grief over the fact that I never got a chance to see him or even know if he was being treated the right way."

• • •

In this chapter, we've explored a variety of circumstances in which we lose our pets and the uncertainty and helplessness we often experience as we navigate their end of life. It's difficult to live peacefully with uncertainty and accept our powerlessness in the face of death. This existential challenge has always been a part of the human condition. We crave agency, but we can't entirely control our fate or the fate of the animals we love. The popular Serenity Prayer offers a clear-headed perspective about learning to recognize what we can and cannot control: "God, grant me the serenity to accept the things I cannot change, the courage to change the things I can, and the wisdom to know the difference."[8]

Of course, recognizing the difference between what we can and cannot change is easier said than done. It's also exceedingly difficult to predict or control how our grief will unfold. Grief resides in a liminal space, or one in which the past, present, and future commingle. You no longer have your pet by your side, so the present may seem like a hellish place, dominated by a longing for what was. The future is unknown and may also seem terribly bleak, and you would probably give anything to turn back the clock and have your pet with you once again.

Yet this is not possible, and many questions might arise as you navigate your sorrow. How can you manage all the unruly, painful emotions that come in death's wake? Is the intense pain you feel normal, and how long will it take before you begin to feel better? Pet loss is a confusing experience, and my goal in the coming chapters is to offer some clarity on the emotional, physical, and spiritual challenges you might encounter on your journey.

CHAPTER 3

Life-Changing, Universe-Shifting Grief

I met Elaine at my pet loss support group not long after her dog Harvey, a six-year-old corgi, had died. Her story has stayed with me because it speaks so strongly to the intense grief that many people experience when they lose a beloved pet.

As sometimes happens, Elaine endured multiple losses that culminated in Harvey's tragic death. Her fiancé, who had adopted Harvey and his brother, Stanley, when they were puppies, died unexpectedly of a massive heart attack. "I kind of felt like a widow with two young children," Elaine said.

But the hardships kept coming. Two years after her fiancé died, Stanley ruptured a disc in his back. Elaine rushed him to an emergency veterinarian, who recommended surgery and gave Stanley a fifty-fifty chance of recovery. Elaine opted for the procedure, and Stanley rallied for a while, but she eventually decided to euthanize him. "That was January of 2011," Elaine said. "January fifth, to be exact, because you remember that stuff."

That's when Elaine's bond with Harvey really began to grow. "Harvey always had to be touching me," she recalled. "It was almost like he knew that he had lost my fiancé and his brother and that I was all he had left. After his brother died, he became more attached to me. I think he was frightened during his brother's illness, not knowing what was going on."

Together, Elaine and Harvey survived their losses. They were happy, and their bond deepened, in part because they'd been through so much together. "It was such an intense feeling I had for Harvey," Elaine said. "In fact, I remember looking at him the night before he died and saying to myself how much I loved him. I just loved that dog so much. I'd never felt that kind of love for a pet. With humans, there's deception, sometimes subterfuge. But with dogs, it's all honesty. It's unconditional love you can have with a pet, and I really think you can't have that for anything else, not even your own child."

But then, in the span of an hour, everything changed.

It was a Saturday morning, and as usual, Elaine and Harvey began their day with a walk through the neighborhood. Later that morning, one of Elaine's friends dropped by, and the two chatted over some coffee, then decided to go out for a quick bite to eat. When they returned home, Elaine discovered Harvey's lifeless body. His head was trapped inside a plastic bag. Her friend had apparently brought a plastic bag with a treat in it and left it out somewhere. Harvey had found it, went after the treat, and suffocated.

For months after Harvey's sudden death, Elaine was consumed by pain. Her grief was very physical. She said her body felt like it was on fire, as if she was being stabbed repeatedly. Every waking moment was painful. She tried to find help to ease her pain. She attended my pet loss support group and worked with a counselor. Her daughter was supportive, but Elaine said that most people didn't understand how she felt and tended to be dismissive of her loss, telling her to "get over it."

When I asked her to reflect on how Harvey's death changed her life, Elaine paused in thought, then homed in on the fragility of her emotions and the fear that had crept into her life.

"I always thought of myself as a resilient person," she said. "And I think I was. I've dealt with lots and lots of hardships in my life, and I was able to overcome them. In fact, I used to have that on my résumé, you know, 'able to overcome obstacles.' But Harvey's death just shattered everything. It shattered all that strength and ability in me. I know I still have some resilience in some areas, but it's weak. Getting a dog is buying a future heartache. I understand the life cycle, and I can handle that. I know I'll be sad and that I'll mourn when I lose them. But I've never gotten over the sudden loss of Harvey. It still hurts when I think about him. I worry about the pets I have now, that something will happen to them. So that's one thing that's changed in me. I was never like that before."

Elaine's story is emblematic of the intense, overwhelming pain that can follow the loss of a pet. The shock of discovering Harvey's lifeless body upset every aspect of her life. Her world spun out of control, and her life was transformed as she came to appreciate how vulnerable we all are to death's unpredictable arrival.

Life is full of loss. We all grapple with losing possessions, people, places, and animals we love. Most of the time, we manage to navigate our losses with resilience and relative calm. Our hearts hurt, yet we stumble through our days until our most intense sorrow eases and we gradually return to a sense of normalcy. We're sad to lose our animal friends, and we miss them terribly. But we survive, and most of us eventually welcome new animals into our hearts.

But some losses are life-altering. In the words of therapist Megan Devine, "There are losses that rearrange the world. Deaths that change the way you see everything, grief that tears everything down. Pain that transports you to an entirely different universe, even while everyone else thinks nothing has really changed."[1]

Elaine suffered this kind of shattering, soul-shaking grief when she lost Harvey so suddenly, and I've encountered many people who've had similar experiences. Like Elaine, they struggled to make it through their day. Sleeplessness, exhaustion, disorientation, physical aches and pains, uncontrollable weeping, hopelessness, and a tangled confluence of sorrow, guilt, and anger permeated their lives.

If you've experienced grief this intense, you might look in the mirror and hardly recognize yourself—this weepy, angry, guilt-ridden, out-of-control person. You might feel an overwhelming and constant longing for your pet. Such yearning is like an elastic cord that pulls you back to your sorrow with every reminder of your animal. You might see a dog who looks like your dog and begin crying uncontrollably. At this point in your journey, memories of your pet may bring no joy but only remind you of their absence. You might even believe you'll never feel happy again.

Such thoughts and feelings usually ease with time, though the transition from aching sorrow to joyful memories usually occurs gradually, sometimes over many years. This change begins with hope. Bryan, the young man I mentioned in the last chapter, learned a great deal about resilience and hope after his dog Ringo died. "The next time I have this happen, I guess I'll be a little wiser in that I'll know, 'You will get through this,'" Bryan said. "When my dog died, I remember I just wanted the pain to go away. I could not imagine how it was going to go away. I had this feeling right here [gestures to his chest]. Somebody else in the group described it too. They said something like, 'The world is going to be different forever now, and I'm going to walk around with this hole in my chest forever.' Now, after some time has passed and after attending the group, I think a lot of getting through life has to do with hope.... Having survived Ringo's loss will help me next time."

Although grief is common to all human beings, it's a difficult topic to pin down and understand with clarity. Psychologists who study grief have tried, primarily by creating theoretical models of grief intended to capture precisely what happens when we lose a loved one or suffer some other disturbing and life-changing event. Grief models can be helpful, but as we'll see in later chapters, they can also mislead us and don't always allow for the unique ways that grief can unfold in our lives.

My goal in this chapter is to offer a comprehensive overview of the human experience of grief. Many commonalities exist between the grief for the loss of a human loved one and grief for a pet, but there are also important differences, and I've adapted my observations about grief to the loss of an animal companion.

Grief Is Not a Single Emotion

We typically talk about grief as if it were a single emotion, but psychologists consider it a *complex emotion*, meaning it's a collection of at least two identifiable feelings. These include shock, disbelief, numbness, sorrow, fear, anger, anxiety, envy, self-pity, relief, joy, guilt, and shame, among others. Such feelings can come and go quickly, making it hard to discern what you're feeling at any moment.

Grief Is Physical

A few years back, I came across a newspaper story about a sixty-two-year-old woman who'd suffered stress-induced cardiomyopathy—a condition often referred to as broken heart syndrome—when her Yorkshire terrier died.[2] In another story, a sixteen-year-old girl became depressed and developed a rash on her hands after her King Charles spaniel died.[3] Within twenty-four hours, her health worsened so drastically that she became unable to swallow food and water. She was admitted to a psychiatric hospital, where her condition improved only when she was able to talk about the loss of her dog with a therapist.

Grief for the loss of an animal can pack a powerful physical blow. People who've attended my pet loss support group often describe their grief in physical terms. Many say they feel as if a hole has opened in their chest or their heart has been torn out. Because our relationships with our pets are strongly physical, such reactions make perfect sense. We stroke, cuddle, and hold our pets close to our hearts, day in and day out, often for years. When they're gone—when their beautiful, expressive faces and warm bodies are no longer with us—we feel utterly bereft.

Grief, then, is not just an emotional challenge but a highly physical, whole-body experience. Because the loss of a loved one is very stressful, it affects our bodies like any other stressful event. Inflammation increases, exacerbating existing health problems and potentially causing new ones. Our immune systems also take a hit, increasing the chance of illness and infection. Our blood pressure tends to rise, increasing the risk of blood clots. Tightness in the chest and throat, difficulty breathing, an upset stomach or nausea, loss of appetite, headaches, general aches and pains, disrupted sleep, and lethargy are also common physical responses to losing a loved one.

Neurological research shows that emotional pain affects the same regions of the brain as physical pain.[4] Consequently, another common feature of grief is mental fog, which is characterized by an inability to process new information, slowness in thought, an overall sense of confusion, forgetfulness, and difficulty making decisions. Brain fog is one way our bodies protect us from pain. Drifting around in a mental fog makes the unbearable bearable because it helps us protect us from external stimulation and gives us a chance to heal.

Although it serves a useful purpose, the fog of grief and the lethargy that accompanies it can make it hard to function in basic ways. Even mundane tasks might seem insurmountable. This kind of grief is utterly consuming. When her husband and daughter died within months of each other, writer Joan Didion described this aspect of her grief in the book *The Year of Magical Thinking*:

> Dolphins. . .had been observed refusing to eat after the death of a mate. Geese had been observed reacting to such a death by flying and calling, searching until they themselves became disoriented and lost. Human beings, I read but did not need to learn, showed similar patterns of response. They searched. They stopped eating. They forgot to breathe. They grew faint

from lowered oxygen, they clogged their sinuses with unshed tears and [developed] obscure ear infections. They lost concentration. They lost cognitive ability on all scales. . . . They forgot their own telephone numbers and showed up at airports without picture ID. They fell sick, they failed, they even . . . died[5]

How long does such fogginess and disorientation last? It's different for everyone. The best you can do is to ask for help from family and friends when you need it. Simplify your life. Prioritize what needs to get done and let go of the rest. Be gentle and patient with yourself. Allow yourself the time and space you need to find your way through the fog of grief until you begin to regain your footing.

Grief Is Social

When we think about grief, most of us tend to see it as a highly personal experience, or something that takes place in our minds and hearts. But this perception is only partly true and overlooks the pivotal influence of our social interactions on our grief.

If you've lost a pet, did the people in your life respond with sympathy, warmth, and patience? Did friends and family members send condolence cards or flowers, as you would expect when a human loved one is lost? Did others continue to offer a sympathetic ear, even when your grief went on for weeks or months? If you're active in a religious community, did you find sympathetic support from your leadership and fellow congregants? If you answered yes to these questions, consider yourself lucky because many people who've lost a pet struggle to find patient, consistent sympathy in their social circles.

Some people claim that the loss of a pet requires less support than the loss of a person—a belief that's implied in comments such as "he was *just* a dog" (or a cat, bird, turtle, fish, and so on). You might be advised to get another pet to feel better, as if one pet can easily replace another. Such comments reflect a bias against animals that's deeply embedded in Western society. It's also likely that people who say things like this have never enjoyed a loving relationship with an animal companion. They simply don't have the experience to understand what you're going through.

Many of us grieve alone for fear of being judged by others, and such isolation tends to exacerbate our grief. I'll return to this important topic in chapter 5, which explores the cultural dimensions of losing a pet. *Just an Animal,* the third book in the series, also explores the social experiences that are common to people who love animals and grieve their loss.

Grief Is Unpredictable

Scholars who study grief describe the experience as emotional oscillation.[6] Grief has a wavelike quality that's characterized by swings between emotional highs and lows. You might struggle with deep feelings of sadness before cycling through a host of "what if" and "if only" thoughts when reflecting on the loss of your pet, then grow angry with yourself or someone else for failing to prevent your pet's illness or injury, and then feel relief that your pet is no longer suffering—all within the space of a single day or even a few minutes. You might feel terribly sad for weeks, then one day wake to a strange sense of peacefulness and love for your pet, only to plunge back into despair by nightfall. Positive feelings are part of grief. It's as if our hearts seek balance simply to keep on beating.

Grief, by its very nature, is unsettling. Life can seem unbalanced and precarious when you've lost a pet who was an important part of your daily routine, and grief's unpredictability can make it hard to adjust to your new normal. Chaplain Lisa Irish writes, "Grief's unpredictability is one of our biggest challenges. We have no control over our emotions, other people, or the new world without our loved one in it. We seek order and we find chaos. We seek a logical progression and find constant change."[7]

We can't predict how grief will unfold because every journey is unique. Yet for most people, it tends to be most intense either before or soon after a loss and eases with time. A man who attended my pet loss support group for more than a year after losing his cat described this phenomenon well. He said it was as if the waves of grief stayed just as high as they did when he first lost his cat, but as time passed those waves became farther apart. The time between those waves gave him a much-needed sense of normalcy and a chance to reflect calmly on his journey. Learning to grieve is about learning to ride those waves of grief.

It's important to trust your grieving process. Rather than fighting these waves, let them take you. Stay present to whatever feelings arise. Grieve. Wail or cry. Rage against the injustice of your loss. Allow yourself to feel your feelings. Remember that with every wave that comes, you're moving forward on your journey. You're not stuck. If grief is an ocean—sometimes calm, sometimes rough and wild—then you're the swimmer, and you're making progress with every good day and every wave of sorrow that washes through your heart.

Grief Takes Time

Just as grief refuses to be put on a schedule, it also doesn't respect deadlines. Grief takes time—sometimes a lot of time. For many, sorrow for the loss of a pet never disappears completely. That's the trade-off for loving well.

Yet even when we acknowledge that we can't rush ourselves to feeling better, we tend to be impatient with our sadness. In our hectic, deadline-driven world, we feel compelled to set a timeline for our recovery. Some people are genuinely concerned that something is wrong with them because they're still grappling with intense pain a few weeks or months after their pet's death. Certainly, no one wants to linger in the intolerable pain of intense grief, and it's understandable that we want to get back to normal as quickly as possible. But every loss is different. Who is to say whether you'll need three weeks, three months, or three years (or more) for your pain to ease? Everyone grieves differently, and it does more harm than good to set arbitrary deadlines for feeling better.

There's truth in the saying that time heals all wounds, but the journey of grief is more nuanced than that. Time may not be enough. It's what unfolds over time that can shape the way your loss plays out in the long run—the way you accept or reject your feelings; the extent to which you allow these feelings to unfold and be fully present with them; and the opportunities you have to share your story with others. If you're actively grieving for a pet, be patient with yourself. Try not to set arbitrary deadlines or expectations for how you should feel from one day to the next. Grief rarely turns out as we expect it to, even if you've said goodbye to many animals in the past. The way you grieved for one pet may be very different than what you're experiencing now.

You Can't Get Around Grief

Psychologist Earl Grollman observes that "the only cure for grief is to grieve."[8] You can try to get around it, but grief will inevitably find its way into your mind and body, like a splinter working its way into your skin. You might attempt to lose yourself in work, school, family obligations, or other activities—anything to keep from engaging directly with your sorrow, guilt, and anger. Frenetic busyness may work for a while and can give you a much-needed break from the hard work of grieving, but there's a difference between taking a temporary respite from your grief and setting your feelings aside altogether.

Lillian, a vet tech student, offered some insight into this dynamic after losing her cat, Freddie. "When I first lost Freddie, I threw myself into my schoolwork," Lillian said. "It was a way of coping. And then I got into a practice of meditation and yoga. But I was just going through the motions. I think staying busy was a form of denial because I wasn't really processing my grief. I was just covering it up with all this activity. But underneath, I was just sad all the time. I learned that there's a difference between being in a moment of sadness, in a particular place or time, and just being deeply, always sad. I had to learn to be OK with that. I had to accept my sadness and not try to pretend I didn't feel it. I also had to get over the guilt because sometimes I felt like I was a bad person because I wanted to be happy and move forward."

Nursing a broken heart is hard work, and most of us need to attend to our grief a little bit at a time. If you're super busy like most people, you might struggle to slow down and tend to your grief. Deadlines and responsibilities at work and school don't stop, and our obligations at home also don't simply disappear. This is why self-compassion, self-care, and patience are vitally important when you're grieving.

Grief Sometimes Begins Before a Loss

Chapter 2 briefly reviewed what is commonly referred to as *anticipatory grief*, or grief that occurs before a loss. To further explicate what anticipatory grief looks like, I'd like to turn to an understanding of grief you're probably familiar with: the five stages of grief from psychologist Elisabeth Kübler-Ross. A pioneer in grief studies, Kübler-Ross introduced this theoretical understanding of grief in 1969 in the bestseller *On Death and Dying*.[9]

The five stages model was revolutionary in its day. In recent decades, however, it has fallen out of favor among grief experts, in part because we often experience emotions not included in the model. The model is also considered too rigid because grief doesn't proceed in an orderly, stepwise fashion as the model seems to imply. Despite its limitations, the five stages model nonetheless offers an astute understanding of the human experience of grief, and it's especially well suited for framing anticipatory grief. This is due to the little-known fact that the model is based on Kübler-Ross's interviews and observations with cancer patients as they contemplated their own impending deaths. Although contemplating your own death is different than contemplating the imminent loss of a pet, the experiences described by the model still hold value. Following is a summary of the five stages model in the context of pet loss.

Denial

Denying a pet's death or loss is straightforward—you simply can't believe your animal is going to die. Denial may be especially common if your pet's physical decline is rapid or they're severely injured. You might cling to any sliver of hope your veterinarian offers, spending thousands of dollars on the latest medical intervention with the hope that you can extend your pet's life by a few days, weeks, or months. Denial can also unfold over a long period of time when you're caring for an old or sick pet. Animals often appear to rally during their physical decline, only to fade quickly. The final weeks of a pet's life may be a roller coaster of emotional highs and lows in which your hopes for recovery surge, only to be dashed overnight, leaving you feeling angry, hopeless, and depleted. The same dynamic may unfold if you're faced with the need to relinquish your pet because of an impending move, a decline in your own physical health, and many other unwelcome scenarios.

Anger

Anger provides structure and focus for an uncontrollable tangle of emotions. As you review the interconnected events that have led to your pet's decline or the need to relinquish them, you might feel angry about what you perceive as poor decisions, if not outright negligence. You might be angry with yourself, friends, family, medical care providers, and even your pet ("How could you leave me?"). You might also feel angry with God, the universe, or the disease itself. Pain lurks beneath anger, and you might hold tight to your anger so you don't feel so sad.

Bargaining

Like anger, bargaining is an attempt to impose order on loss. You want life returned to what it was. You want your pet restored. You want to go back in time to the point when you're able to recognize your pet's illness more quickly or stop the accident from happening. Backed into a corner with no good options, you might beg God or the universe to give you more time with your pet, just a few precious hours or days to make up for those occasions when you weren't as attentive as you wish you had been or were short-tempered with your animal.

Depression

At some point in your animal's illness and decline—or in situations when you know you have no choice but to rehome your pet—you're likely to be hit hard by the reality of what you're facing. You know your pet is going to die or that you'll need to rehome them, and it hurts like hell. When you experience such intense sadness, you might believe these dark feelings will last forever, that there will never be any way to escape and return to normal. An overwhelming sense of hopelessness and despair may set in.

Acceptance

This stage is about accepting the reality that you're going to lose your pet and recognizing that this new reality will be permanent. You've come to the point of accepting the inevitability of your pet's death or the circumstances that are forcing you to relinquish them. At some point, you just can't argue with the facts. But acceptance does not mean that you're OK with your loss. It has nothing to do with how you *feel* about your animal's loss, but how you *think* about the loss. Of all the stages in Kübler-Ross's model, acceptance is the most misunderstood. Many people falsely equate acceptance with a sense of emotional calm and detachment. Yet this was not Kübler-Ross's intention, and I'll explore this aspect of the five stages and similar models of grief in greater detail in the chapter 6.

Every Journey of Grief Is Unique

While this discussion has focused on grief's common attributes, grief is as unique as the people who experience it. Many factors influence the way we respond to the loss of a loved one. For example, a study of US pet keepers found that grief is more difficult and long lasting when we're socially isolated, when an animal plays a crucial role in helping us cope with an illness or disability, and when it's compounded by other concurrent losses or stressful life events.[10]

To conclude this chapter, I'll briefly review some of the circumstances that might impact your grief journey. These observations are offered only as generalizations. For example, the idea that men process and express their feelings differently from women may not always hold true. I encourage you to weigh these observations against your personal experience and how you've responded to hardships in the past.

The quality of your attachment
The nature of your relationship with your pet can profoundly impact the intensity of your grief. Was your pet your heart animal, or one with whom you were particularly close? You might have kept dozens of animals in your lifetime and loved them all, but most people can identify one or two animals who were especially important to them. When you lose a pet you consider your soul mate, it's like losing a part of yourself.

The age of your pet when they died or were lost can also complicate matters. If your pet was very old, you might be able to console yourself with the knowledge that they led a long, full life. But if your pet died or was otherwise lost at a young age, you might feel angry and cheated because the loss of a young pet feels at odds with the natural order of the world. This can be problematic with purebred animals, who tend to have lifelong health issues, or those who are raised by irresponsible breeders and have serious health problems throughout their lives.

The circumstances of the loss

The circumstances of a pet's loss can have a profound effect on the intensity and trajectory of your grief journey. Was your pet's death sudden, violent, or harrowing? Did you feel responsible for their death or loss? Were you attending to your old, disabled, or sick pet for a long time before their death? Were you forced to euthanize your pet because you couldn't afford treatment or because your animal had unresolvable behavioral issues? Similarly, were you forced to relinquish your pet against your will? All these scenarios can intensify your grief.

The co-occurrence of other stressful events

I've encountered many pet keepers who lost a pet while they were in the throes of other highly stressful events, such as the death of a family member or close friend, the loss of their job or home, a divorce, relocation, and so on. Sometimes the death of a pet can push you past your limits, and grief that has accumulated through multiple losses might overwhelm you. Dealing with multiple crises might force you to ignore or deny the grief you feel for your pet.

Your gender, personality, and overall health

Your gender and personality may shape the way you respond to your pet's death. In the West, men are socially conditioned to keep their feelings to themselves, while women generally feel more comfortable expressing their feelings and reaching out for help. Men might also respond to their grief as if it were a problem to be solved, and many will get busy with practical activities. Regardless of their gender, however, some people confront their grief head-on while others prefer a less overt and more contemplative approach to processing their feelings.

Your overall physical and mental health can also impact your ability to weather your loss. If you suffer from low self-esteem or struggle with depression, you might fall rapidly into despair. Grief can feel a lot like depression, so it can be difficult to discern the difference. Similarly, addictive behaviors tend to increase after a loss and can hamper your ability to engage with your feelings. If you struggle with physical challenges, such as chronic illnesses or pain, your condition may grow worse after you lose your pet because of sleep interruptions, poor appetite, and intense sadness. Finally, if you have serious health issues and your body and mind are fragile, the death of your pet might remind you of your own vulnerability, which can exacerbate your grief.

Your prior experience with death
Another important consideration is your prior experience with death. If you've never lost a loved one, you might feel bewildered by all the decisions that need to be made at the end of your pet's life. You might also be confused by the tangle of physical, emotional, and spiritual challenges that come with grief. If you've dealt with death before, especially the death of a pet, you're likely to respond in much the same way that you did then, or in the way your parents or other adults modeled grief.

. . .

Grief is a natural response to a significant loss or other distressing, life-changing event. It's a complex emotion consisting of many different feelings as well as physical sensations. It doesn't respect deadlines and is unpredictable. It tends to ease with time, although it may never go away completely. Grief can also begin before an animal is lost. Every loss is unique, and every individual's journey of grief will be unique to them and the time and circumstances in which the loss occurs.

In the next chapter, we'll focus on an emotion that is especially common among people who've lost a pet: guilt. Almost every pet keeper I've ever met experiences at least some regret for the choices they made as they navigated their pet's end of life, and some are racked by guilt for years. Guilt is very difficult to set aside, so it's worth pondering this powerful emotion, its root causes, and the various ways we might seek forgiveness for our perceived mistakes.

CHAPTER 4

Guilt and Forgiveness

Dwight Briggs attended my pet loss support group regularly for two or three years. He was a reliable and conscientious man who would often text me to let me know if he couldn't make it to the monthly meeting. Dwight and his wife lived in the country, where large colonies of feral cats were common. They fed the cats, trapped some of them, and worked with local veterinarians who run catch-and-release sterilization clinics to help control the feral cat population. If they found friendly cats, usually kittens, Dwight and his wife tried to find permanent homes for them, and they sometimes adopted the cats themselves.

Dwight came to the group after losing his home in a fire. It wasn't the loss of his home and possessions that troubled Dwight the most. Possessions can be replaced. Lives cannot. It was the deaths of five rescue cats—Ricky, Lucy, Little Boo, Missy, and Scooter—that weighed heavily on his heart.

The fire started on Dwight's back porch late on a winter evening when a heat lamp he had set up to keep the cats warm had fallen over. Dwight had trained and served for six years as a volunteer firefighter, and he tried to put out the fire with a garden hose. "But it's different when it's your house," he said. "Everything happened so fast. I was trying to put the fire out, but I just wasn't thinking."

At one point, Dwight tried to go back into the house through the back door, but it was locked. In the following passage, he describes this hellish experience:

> I couldn't get back in. I could see my wife in the kitchen, but I couldn't get her to open the door. She was probably calling the fire department, but I was beating on the door, trying to get her to come to the door. I tried to knock the door down. Couldn't get it down. I saw her go back in the main part of the house, and all I could think was, "I'll never see her again." I was just helpless, completely helpless. It was like everything was moving in slow motion. Finally, she let me in. I asked where the cats were, but she didn't know. I couldn't find them anywhere. I went to the back part of the house where I knew the cats liked to hide. There was lots of smoke, and the fire was heavy. I crawled on my hands and knees. I looked everywhere. I couldn't find the cats anywhere. I couldn't go into the main part of the house because it was fully engulfed in fire. I came back out after I couldn't breathe anymore.

Dwight suffered second-degree burns on his hands and shoulders and was diagnosed with post-traumatic stress disorder (PTSD). When he was released from the hospital, he and his wife had only the clothes on their backs. But help came from all around, sometimes in unexpected ways. Dwight's veterinarian donated five tiny coffins for the five cats who were lost, and nearly two dozen of his coworkers from his trucking company came out to help dig graves. Dwight and his wife still had some feral kittens hanging around their property, and the veterinarian took them in, gave them their shots, and, with the help of Dwight's feral cat rescue group, found homes for them. Gradually, the couple began to rebuild their lives.

Yet Dwight's guilt was relentless. For months, he was consumed with thoughts about every detail of that tragic night. He blamed himself for the fire because he'd set up the heat lamp that had fallen over. He'd also overlooked Scooter's body, which was later discovered wedged behind the hot tub on the back porch. In the frantic moments when he was searching for the cats, he'd looked all around the hot tub except in the one spot where Scooter was hiding. His thoughts settled into a familiar pattern. *If only* he'd secured that heater better, he said to himself, the fire might never have started. *If only* he'd looked for the cats rather than trying to put the fire out, they might still be alive. Overwhelmed with guilt, Dwight struggled to make peace with his actions on the night of the fire and the role he played in the cats' deaths.

I've met many people who insist they were responsible for their pet's death even when it seemed obvious that they were not. Yet logic doesn't reside comfortably with grief. Even when you acknowledge intellectually that there was nothing you could have done to save your pet, you might still blame yourself. You might tell yourself repeatedly that if only you'd made a different choice, your pet would still be with you.

In the bestseller *The Year of Magical Thinking*, Joan Didion noticed the fanciful, illogical thinking she experienced following the deaths of her husband and daughter. "I was incapable of thinking rationally," she wrote. "I was thinking as small children think, as if my thoughts or wishes had the power to reverse the narrative, change the outcome."[1] What Didion calls "magical thinking" reflects an anguished need to rearrange the past, restore the life that has been lost, and erase the overwhelming guilt that compels you to believe that a different outcome was possible if only you'd made a different choice. No matter what the circumstances of your pet's death or how hard you tried to keep them healthy and happy, you might still harbor a lingering feeling that you somehow could have saved them. You might repeatedly review the circumstances of your animal's death, recalling every detail, every word or action, to discover the precise moment when you could have saved your pet. You might reprimand yourself with constant self-talk, thinking "I should have been there" or "I should have seen the signs."

Of the many fleeting feelings that constitute the complex emotion of grief, guilt is one of the most common among people who've lost an animal companion. It's also the emotion that tends to linger the longest. Guilt feels awful, but it can also be empowering. It helps us impose order on the unpredictability of life, providing a distraction from the sorrow and despair that reside just below the surface of our consciousness. But self-blame can easily become an obsession, making it difficult for you to connect with your happy memories. At some point, you might realize that this whirlpool of guilt is impeding your life and your healing.

So what drives this repetitive pattern? Why does guilt tend to grab hold of us and refuse to let go? It's worth understanding the deeper mechanisms at work here, especially when you keep coming back to the same unavoidable conclusion—that you were powerless to change the outcome and your pet is gone.

Guilt, Powerlessness, and the Human Condition

Humans are blessed with both foresight and creativity. We can imagine the future we want to create, and we can also strive to create the future we imagine. We tend to spend a lot of time and energy planning for the future, yet those plans don't typically include death. Often, we simply pretend that death doesn't exist, and it can be a terrifying shock when it arrives unexpectedly.

Powerlessness, our constant struggle against death, and the unpredictability of life are at the heart of the human condition. We despise chaos and crave agency. We attempt to exert power over our lives in ways as simple as choosing what to have for breakfast or as complex as deciding to change jobs or get married. With each of these choices, we're exerting control over our lives. Like a soothing tonic, making both daily choices and major decisions creates the comforting illusion that we have control over our world, both in the present and in the future.

Death can destroy all of that in an instant. It can rob us of our sense of agency. It leaves us struggling to live in a world that no longer makes sense and over which we have little to no control.

Framed in this way, the reasons many of us are so easily captivated by intractable guilt after losing a pet become clear. If you can assume responsibility for their death—even in the remotest way, through ignorance, negligence, or both—then the events surrounding their death make sense. You can then assure yourself that you are not powerless, that the events that led to the loss of your pet could have been controlled and death could have been avoided, if only you had acted differently.

The alternative to this cause-and-effect perspective is frightening. An unpredictable world full of random accidents, disease, misery, and senseless death over which we have little or no control is simply too terrifying to contemplate. Most of us would much prefer to live in a world where we have power and control as long as we're vigilant and responsible. Humans abhor feeling powerless, so we look for something we missed, something we could have done, to reinforce the possibility that we had the power to avoid death but failed to use it.

We also go to great lengths to forestall death's arrival. Yet we cannot. There's an ancient tale that speaks to this unavoidable truth. The tale first appeared in the Jewish Talmud, which was written in Babylonia (Mesopotamia) about 1,500 years ago, and Muslim Sufi literature also includes a version of this well-known tale. Titled "Appointment in Samarra," this simple but chilling story goes as follows:

> There was a merchant in Baghdad who sent his servant to market to buy provisions, and in a little while the servant came back, white and trembling, and said, "Master, just now when I was in the marketplace I was jostled by a woman in the crowd, and when I turned I saw it was Death that had jostled

me. She looked at me and made a threatening gesture. Now, lend me your horse, and I will ride away from this city and avoid my fate. I will go to Samarra, and there Death will not find me."

The merchant lent him his horse, and the servant mounted it, and he dug his spurs in its flanks and as fast as the horse could gallop, he went.

Then the merchant went down to the marketplace, and he saw Death disguised as a woman standing in the crowd, and he came to her and said, "Why did you make a threatening gesture to my servant when you saw him this morning?"

"That was not a threatening gesture," the woman said. "It was only an expression of surprise. I was astonished to see him in Baghdad, for I had an appointment with him tonight in Samarra."[2]

As this story illustrates, we're willing to work very hard to escape death. We also avoid thinking and speaking about it. But then without warning, death arrives. The loss of a loved one, whether human or animal, can raise the specter of death, and we often struggle in those moments to quell the fear and anxiety that arises in our hearts.

To circle back to the primary focus of this chapter, the guilt many people experience following the death of their pet is symptomatic of the existential crisis that lies at the heart of the human condition. It reflects the tension between our deep-seated desire to preserve and extend life and our inability to do so. Death cheats us all of what we want most—more life.

The point is that the unfounded guilt described here can be understood as an emotional manifestation of our anxiety about death and our discomfort with powerlessness. The connection between these phenomena may seem nebulous, and it can be difficult to appreciate how our innate anxiety about death and our need for agency shape our emotions and our behavior. Yet I believe that understanding this connection can be helpful and even liberating. When we accept our limitations, we might begin to see ourselves as a small part of the cosmos and participants in the miracle of life and death. Many spiritual traditions and secular philosophies emphasize the need to accept death, ambiguity, uncertainty, and helplessness as a part of life. They call on us to relinquish our illusion of control and be vulnerable and open to what life can teach us. This is the path of humility and grace. As noted by rabbi and theologian Rami Shapiro, "Life is not something we control or manage. Life is something that happens to us, in us, and through us. We respond to what life brings; we do not control what it brings."[3]

Guilt Versus Remorse

When Dwight lost five cats in the house fire, he grieved for all of them. But he took the loss of one of those cats, a tiny feline named Scooter, especially hard.

Dwight found Scooter as a kitten when she was dragging herself around with her forelegs under his back porch. She'd either been attacked by an animal or had an accident because her spine was broken. "I saved that cat's life," Dwight said. "The vet wanted to put her down. I understood where she was coming from because most people wouldn't take the time and expense to care for a crippled cat like that. But I chose to keep Scooter. I took good care of her. She meant a lot to me."

The fact that Scooter had special needs contributed greatly to Dwight's sorrow. "That cat was like a child," he said. "Most animals, you feed and water them, and they can drink and eat by themselves and go to the bathroom on their own. But Scooter really depended on me for everything. I love all the animals I take care of equally, but I guess it was extra hard to lose her because she was so needy. She depended on me, and I let her down."

Many people appear to have a need to nurture other living things, especially those who are injured or have special needs. If you consider yourself a pet parent, losing your animal can feel like losing a child. Your sense of responsibility for your animal may be so strong that you consistently second-guess your decisions regarding their health. You might think that if you'd only paid more attention to the signs of their illness, they would still be alive. Some scholars describe this phenomenon as the "guilt of responsibility."[4]

This observation raises an important point. While most pet keepers use the word *guilt* to describe their feelings after losing a pet, I believe most are actually experiencing remorse. Guilt is defined as "feelings of deserving blame especially for imagined offenses or from a sense of inadequacy."[5] In contrast, remorse is "a gnawing distress arising from a sense of guilt for past wrongs."[6] Guilt is self-focused and concerned with breaking our personal moral code. In contrast, remorse is focused on the sorrow we feel for the harm we've caused others. Guilt may not always lead to acts of atonement, while remorse often prompts a desire to repair the harm we believe we've caused and seek forgiveness from those we've harmed.

Celeste, a vet tech student, was overwhelmed with remorse when her dog, Rambo, was found dead by the side of the road. Celeste had made the difficult decision to leave her abusive husband, but she couldn't afford to take Rambo with her. She knew there was a chance that her husband would neglect or hurt him, which is apparently what happened because her ex had gone on vacation and left Rambo outside to fend for himself. Although she wasn't directly responsible for his death, Celeste nonetheless believed there was more she could have done to protect Rambo. "When I found out Rambo had died, I felt a ton of grief run over me," Celeste said. "I was horrified. I tried to apologize to him. I felt like I failed him because I couldn't take him with me. I felt like I let him down. All I could do was pray that he's up in heaven and has the freedom to run around and do all the things I wished he could have done down here. I hope that Rambo doesn't hold it against me because I couldn't take him with me."

Many scenarios can lead to feelings of remorse when a pet is lost.

Euthanasia can be particularly problematic. As noted earlier, studies have shown that pet keepers who euthanize a pet tend to experience more long-lasting feelings of guilt compared to people whose pets died naturally of disease or old age.[7] Some people also feel remorse because they were short-tempered with their pet near the end of their life or wished they'd spent more time with them.

When we believe we've harmed those we love—especially those who depend on us—the path to self-forgiveness can be very difficult. Yet it's important to remember that our anguish reflects our love for our animal friends. Remorse is only present when compassion is present. Yet we rarely afford ourselves the same compassion, and this seems particularly true of people who enjoy nurturing others and are inclined to put others' needs ahead of their own.

Finding Forgiveness

So what can we do to break the punishing cycle of guilt and remorse that is such a common part of pet loss? As noted earlier in this chapter, accepting our limitations as mortal beings who cannot control the whims of life and death is a good starting point. On a practical level, I typically counsel people who are struggling with remorse to write a letter to their pet, asking for forgiveness.

Helping others by volunteering your time and energy to a cause you believe in can also be very healing. After losing Rambo, Celeste got involved in animal rescue to atone for the mistakes she believed she'd made with Rambo and other animals who'd suffered because of her ex-husband's abuse. "I went into animal rescue because of what I saw Rambo and other animals go through," she said. "It's like seeing an abused child. I can't handle that." Similarly, Dwight found relief for his remorse by doubling down on his volunteer work in feral cat rescue. He attended my pet loss support group for many years, not only to address his grief but to help other attendees with theirs. His presence was wonderfully affirming. He knew the agony of losing a pet, and he understood how remorse can eat away at a person's soul. Perhaps he discovered that by helping others heal from their losses, he was also healing himself.

Rituals can also be helpful when we're seeking forgiveness. I've sometimes conducted a ritual in my pet loss support group in which participants write brief notes to their pets. They express their continuing love and sometimes seek forgiveness. These small pieces of paper are then touched to a candle, and, as the smoke rises, I lead the group in prayers for the pet keeper and their animal. Though simple, rituals like this can be powerfully healing because they help people feel connected to their animal's spirit.

Many people engage in prayer and spiritual reflection when they feel remorse after losing a pet. This was true for Dwight. "Every Sunday when I visit my mother's grave, I ask for the cats' forgiveness," he said. "I've always thought it would help me closure-wise. I thought it would help to know that they're OK wherever they are. Hopefully, they're in heaven. No more pain. Now, I haven't told many people this because most people would think I'm crazy. But one night I was out driving my truck. Driving along by yourself, you get a lot of time to think. And I looked up at the sky, and I asked my mom for a sign to let me know she was OK. I asked for a sign that the cats were OK, too. And at that moment, I saw five shooting stars. In my heart, that was my mom's sign to me, and it gave me a little bit of peace."

Ultimately, the key to finding forgiveness lies with self-compassion. People who regularly practice self-compassion tend to suffer less depression, physical problems, and intractable guilt than those who are self-judging. In one pet loss study, pet keepers who were more oriented toward self-compassion consistently had less anxiety and depression and fewer somatic troubles than those who were self-blaming.[8] Psychological educator and author Kristen D. Neff identified three primary facets of self-compassion: first, self-kindness, or when you avoid judging yourself and instead strive to be considerate and empathetic toward your thoughts and behaviors; second, identifying yourself as part of humanity and understanding that making mistakes and having difficulties is part of being human; and, third, the cultivation of mindfulness, which refers to the ability to be present in a nonjudgmental way in every moment and peacefully acknowledge whatever you're experiencing in that moment.[9] This includes being fully present to painful feelings rather than seeking distractions or stuffing them away.

It's also important to remember that self-compassion is not the same as self-improvement. In the US, many people are quick to jump on the bandwagon of self-improvement when they encounter a challenge. As psychotherapist Francis Weller points out, we often believe "that our weakness or inadequacy, our neediness or our failures are the reasons for our suffering, and if only we could be free of them, we would enter into a state of perfection, [and] all would be well."[10] Our habit of seeing the self as the root of everything positive and negative in our lives is reinforced by our culture, which celebrates individuality and independence. In American society, we're constantly told that we need only set our sights higher and work harder to be happy. Yet the loss of a loved one and the grief that comes with it have little to do with our achievements. Grief requires healing and sometimes redemption, not self-improvement, and this is only possible if we accept ourselves for who we are.

When we forgive ourselves, we recognize our own humanity, accept our imperfections and misjudgments, and honor our struggle to do our best for the animals in our care. We free ourselves from the heavy chains of guilt and remorse and open a space in our hearts where healing and new learning can flourish.

• • •

In the last two chapters, we've taken a close look at what grief for the loss of a pet looks and feels like. We've delved deeply into the human psyche to identify the commonalities of grief and the existential challenges that drive the guilt and remorse that many people experience when they lose a pet. Guilt and remorse are the crucibles of pet loss, a severe test and an agent of change. They're also a test of our spirit, and when we strive to atone for our actions and right a perceived wrong, we can experience profound spiritual growth.

Guilt and remorse—like grief itself—only exist in relation to others. In other words, grief is *relational*, not personal. As I briefly noted in chapter 3, our social experiences can have a profound impact on our grief journeys and our ability to make peace with our losses. Our social world includes our interactions with the people we're closest to, but it also encompasses the social norms about grief at work in our culture and subcultures. In the next chapter, we'll broaden our focus from the individual grieving experience to consider the impact of social norms about grief and the unique cultural challenges of losing a pet in contemporary Western society.

CHAPTER 5

How Culture Shapes Our Grief

Like the US, Japan is a pet-loving society. As of 2025, pets in Japan outnumber children under fifteen years old, a startling statistic that reflects an aging population and the rise in single-person households.[1] Dogs are the most popular pet, with 51 percent of Japanese pet keepers having a canine companion, followed closely by cats at 41 percent. Like their American counterparts, many Japanese regard their animals as family members and often refer to their pets as *uchi-no-ko*, or "our child."

My coauthor Karen and I visited Japan in the spring of 2025, and we were delighted to see people strolling along Kyoto's Kamo River with their dogs in tow, enjoying the sunny weather and beautiful cherry blossoms. The striking shiba inu, a native Japanese breed with a foxlike appearance, was especially common, though we encountered many other breeds, from tiny chihuahuas to enormous Japanese Akitas. We even met a bulldog dressed up in a floral kimono and comfortably seated in a baby carriage, and the man pushing the stroller proudly let us take their picture.

When it comes to the loss of their pets, many Japanese mark their animals' deaths with elaborate public rituals. In the book *Bones of Contention: Animals and Religion in Contemporary Japan*, religious studies scholar Barbara Ambros describes a pet memorial service held at a Buddhist temple in Japan:

> Elderly couples, middle-aged women, and young families with children spill into the hallway and the spacious waiting room, where they can follow the ceremony on a large-screen plasma TV. Overseas patrons halfway around the globe can watch a silent live stream of the ritual over the Internet on the temple's website. Accompanied by a cymbal, the abbot and his assistants recite scriptures and incantations to consecrate stacks of miniature *tōba*, wooden tablets shaped like stupas inscribed with the names of the deceased. . . . As they enter the main hall one by one, two clerics stamp the miniature *tōba* with a seal and read out loud the names of the deceased: "Okano Chocolate, Osaka Pon, Kikuchi Pudding, Maruko Pyonta"—dogs, cats, rabbits, ferrets, hamsters and birds.[2]

In contrast, public rituals memorializing lost pets are exceedingly rare in the US and other developed Western countries. Perhaps this has something to do with our culture's aversion to public displays of grief. Cindy Cline, who helped launch a pet ministry at Unity of Houston in 2017, said that Unity's Animal Kinship Ministry had tried to launch an annual memorial event to commemorate the loss of congregants' pets, but it was poorly attended. It was only when they paired their annual blessing of the animals with a memorial service that attendance improved.

The point is that cultural differences in how people grieve can be stark. In the US and arguably in other Western countries, we tend to pay little attention to the social and cultural forces that shape our grief. We regard grief as a personal experience, or something that occurs solely in our minds and hearts. But this hyperfocus on our internal lives is not universal. Other cultures place much more emphasis on collective rituals of mourning. As noted by psychologist

George Bonanno, "People in non-Western cultures don't pay as much attention to individuals and their feelings. They care more about the interactions between people than about what is going on in any one person's head."[3]

Most understandings of grief in Western society originated in the field of psychology, which is concerned primarily with our personal emotions and sensations. We reviewed some of the common characteristics of grief for the loss of a pet in the last two chapters, and in the next chapter, we'll take a closer look at several psychological grief models. Yet broader perspectives that consider grief from a cultural and subcultural perspective offer interesting insights into the grieving experience. In this chapter, we'll explore the cultural dimensions of grief, past and present. My hope is that this discussion will broaden your perspective on your personal journey and help you understand the unique challenges of losing a pet in the modern age.

Grief as a Social Phenomenon

Grief is universal among human beings and other highly social animals, such as dogs, cats, primates, whales, and elephants, who grieve when a member of their social group is injured or dies. The key word here is *social*. Our worldview and what we consider natural and normal are shaped by the messages we receive from our families, social circles, subcultures, and cultures. Understanding these influences gives us the opportunity to step back from our personal perspectives about grief and reflect on what we've been taught with a critical eye. Do our ideas about grief and the ways we're taught to express our feelings help or hinder our ability to cope with the loss of a loved one?

To explore this question, I'll review a theoretical understanding of grief known as *social constructionism* that originated in the fields of sociology and anthropology. Social constructionism provides insight into a wide variety of human behaviors. The theory maintains that our perception of reality and the meanings we make of our experiences are created collectively or within our social groups. Regarding grief, social constructionism emphasizes the social and cultural influences on the experience of grief that psychological theories tend to ignore. Social scientists assert that our social relationships and dominant cultural norms play a pivotal role in how we respond to a significant loss. In other words, grief is not solely a private, internal experience but a social one that's strongly shaped by the expectations and norms of our families, communities, and cultures.

This perspective raises some thought-provoking questions. Is grief a universal experience? That is, do all people experience the same thing in response to similar events? Does the way we grieve change over time, from one generation to another? What societal expectations shape our ideas about proper ways to grieve and express our feelings? And what are the norms of proper mourning, or those public displays of grief that signal to others that we've suffered a significant loss?

In a chapter titled "Grief" in the scholarly book *The Handbook of the Sociology of Emotions*, social scientists Kathy Charmaz and Melinda Milligan offer some compelling insights into these questions.[4] They assert that although grief is universal among human beings, how we experience and express grief varies across time, place, and culture. To support their position, Charmaz and Milligan cite the work of anthropologist Nancy Scheper-Hughes, who studied the women of Alto do Cruzeiro, Brazil, a community with extremely high rates of infant and child mortality. Scheper-Hughes discovered that women often did not become emotionally attached to their children until they had survived for about five years and, further, that the women did not grieve the deaths of their infants or very young children. Hughes concluded that "emotions do not precede or stand outside of culture; they are a part of culture. . . . Without our cultures, *we simply would not know how to feel*" (emphasis in the original).[5] Although you might find it hard to believe that you wouldn't grieve the loss of an infant or very young child, research like this demonstrates how greatly our beliefs about ourselves are socially constructed and reflect our life circumstances.

Closer to home, the experience of grief and acceptable ways of expressing it have changed greatly in the West over the last century. In the Victorian era, middle-class Americans saw grief as an inevitable and powerful experience that should be embraced with vigor and vitality. Grief was considered an important life event. It was neither shunned nor hidden, though proper and improper ways of expressing one's grief were common. Men were expected to express their emotions energetically, as if ridding themselves of evil spirits, and women were encouraged to share their grief openly and cry on each other's shoulders. Victorian-era women wore black and sometimes an armband or other physical marker, such as a mourning jewel, to signal the loss of a family member. According to Walter R. Houghton, who wrote a book in 1889 about social etiquette in the US, "The deepest mourning is that worn by a widow for her husband. It is worn for two years, sometimes longer. . . . The mourning for a father or mother is worn for one year. . . . Mourning for a brother or sister is worn for six months."[6]

By the middle of the twentieth century, however, most Americans saw grief as decidedly unpleasant and without positive value. Rather than being embraced, grief became something to be avoided, minimized, repressed, and quieted as quickly as possible. In *Death, Grief, and Mourning*, which was published in 1965, social anthropologist Geoffrey Gorer observed that public mourning in the US and England was rejected, and this rejection was the "result of the increasing pressure of a new 'ethical duty to enjoy oneself,' a novel 'imperative to do nothing which might diminish the enjoyment of others.' . . . The contemporary trend was 'to treat mourning as morbid self-indulgence, and to give social admiration to the bereaved who hide their grief so fully that no one would guess anything had happened.'"[7] Psychotherapist Megan Devine makes a similar observation. "Our culture sees grief as a kind of malady: a terrifying, messy emotion that needs to be cleaned up and put behind us as soon as possible," Devine writes. "As a result, we have outdated beliefs around how long grief should last and what it should look like. We see it as something to overcome, something to fix, rather than something to tend or support."[8]

Today, the unstated expectation in many Western countries—and, perhaps, especially in the US—is that we must put our losses behind us and tamp down our painful feelings. Like the Bobby McFerrin song "Don't Worry, Be Happy," our culture celebrates people who are happy, upbeat, and meet life's challenges with optimism and pluck. Redemption stories with happy endings abound in American culture. In keeping with this insistently optimistic mentality, we're expected to recover quickly from our losses and avoid displaying our sadness and despair in public.

Many of us also have trouble carving time out of our busy schedules to attend to our grief. Many of us work long hours, hold down multiple jobs, and spend hours commuting. Throw in the challenges of childcare, pet care, and the basic demands of life—preparing food, maintaining a home, and squeezing in some time for hobbies and distractions—and it's no wonder we have no time to grieve when we lose a loved one.

This is not necessarily a matter of choice. Our workplaces rarely give us the time we need to handle the demands that death places on us, from making decisions about after-death body care to arranging a memorial for the deceased. Some people are granted a few days of bereavement leave from work for the death of a close relative such as a parent or child (typically only five days), but many of us are expected to get back to work without delay. The situation is worse when the deceased is an animal. Formal leave for the loss of a companion animal is rare among US employers. I've met a few pet keepers who had sympathetic supervisors who encouraged them to take off a few days from work when their pet died. But what is a few days when your intense pain continues month after month, you can hardly get out of bed in the morning, and you're inclined to burst into tears without warning? The message we receive from our employers is that we need to buck up and get back to work as quickly as possible, even though we may have trouble functioning in even basic ways, especially soon after a loss.

Given our society's discomfort with grief and the tremendous social pressure we all feel to get on with our lives after a loss, it's no wonder that some of us turn to pharmaceuticals to make it through the day. And herein lies another problem with the way we manage grief in our society: the belief that grief is an illness that can be cured.

The Medicalization of Grief

Psychology and psychiatry are branches of medical science, and, like doctors who attend to our physical health, the goal of a clinical counselor, psychologist, psychiatrist, or similar professional is to cure the mentally ill person and restore them to good health. In keeping with this goal, many therapists have been taught to regard grief as something akin to mental illness, a perspective that is still widespread today. As noted by sociologists Charmaz and Milligan, "Western understandings of grief largely emerged from institutionalized medicine and have been granted considerable generality and universality. . . . If at the public level grief has been medicalized, at the private level it has been individualized. At both levels, psychological perspectives have dominated understandings of grief and framed it as an illness to ameliorate by going through a 'normal' progression of stages."[9]

Grief can be intense, so you might seek the help of a counselor to ease your pain and because you worry that you've become clinically depressed. A therapist will typically offer a variety of interventions for your sorrow, from long-term counseling to behavior modification. If your grief is intense and long-lasting, you might be diagnosed as suffering from pathological or complicated grief, and interventions for this diagnosis include pharmaceuticals. In 2013 the American Psychiatric Association added grief to the latest release of the *Diagnostic and Statistical Manual of Mental Disorders* (DSM-5), the main diagnostic guide for mental health professionals.[10] According to this manual, a person who has suffered the loss of a human loved one and is displaying symptoms of major depressive disorder for two weeks can be prescribed antidepressant medicine. The most recent DSM-5, released in March 2022, includes a new diagnostic criterion called *prolonged grief disorder.*

Why is grief included in a manual of mental health disorders? Is grief, in fact, a form of mental illness? Clinical counselor and grief expert Dr. Alan Wolfelt has challenged the inclusion of grief in the DSM-5 and asserts that grief is not an illness or mental health disorder, even when it's long-lasting. In a 2022 blog post, Wolfelt wrote that in forty years of working with grieving people, he has learned that "the normal melancholy of grief often continues well beyond a year. To integrate it into our ongoing lives, grief takes expression (i.e., mourning), the support of others, and an indeterminate amount of time."[11]

I agree with Wolfelt. I've spent decades attending to grieving people, and I strongly advocate for a non-medicalized approach to grief care. I recognize that pharmaceuticals can help grieving people cope and better manage their daily tasks, but I'm skeptical that drugs offer more than short-term benefit. If used for an extended period, they can even be counterproductive. Drugs typically used to treat depression and anxiety can stifle *all* your feelings. This might be expedient if you're struggling to manage basic tasks and responsibilities. But it can also make it difficult to engage with your feelings and make meaning of your loss. As noted earlier, "The only cure for grief is to grieve."[12] But how can you grieve if you don't feel anything?

I also worry that framing grief as a mental health disorder or illness sends the wrong message. Mental illness has long been stigmatized in our society. Positioning grief as a mental health disorder risks exacerbating the dismay and shame grieving people already experience because of their unruly emotions. If we're made to feel ashamed of our grief, we're more likely to ignore our feelings or try to hide them.

When we lose a loved one—especially when that loved one is an animal—we're under tremendous pressure to swallow our sorrow, paste a smile on our faces, get back to work, and perform like rock stars. Elaine's story about her dog Harvey presented in chapter 3 demonstrates the high price we pay for ignoring our pain and trying to quickly resume our normal lives after a difficult loss. At the time of Harvey's death, Elaine was working as an administrative assistant for a C-level executive in a large corporation, and she had always been a top performer. Her job was demanding, fast-paced, and detail-oriented, and there was little tolerance for error. To cope with the demands of her job, Elaine started taking medication for the anxiety and insomnia she experienced after Harvey died. But the drugs, in combination with her intense grief, left her feeling mentally foggy and physically exhausted. One day, she inadvertently deleted an important meeting from her boss's calendar. Her boss was furious, but Elaine didn't feel comfortable sharing the cause of her distraction.

Ultimately, the pressure to perform at work when she could barely function was too much for Elaine. Three months after Harvey died, she decided to retire. "I just couldn't cope anymore," she said. "Every morning and every night driving home from work, I would scream. I would just cry and scream because I was so heartbroken over Harvey's death. It was so senseless and so sudden. I was just unprepared."

Grieving for a Pet in Western Society

The reflections I've shared here are broad and apply to the grief we experience for any loss, from the death of a family member or friend to the loss of a job or marriage. Yet grieving for a pet in the modern West presents some unique challenges that are generally absent when we grieve the loss of a human loved one.

Although we celebrate pet keeping in the modern West, the loss of an animal companion is still widely regarded as a small grief that we should be able to recover from quickly. This is a misperception. I've witnessed firsthand that many people grieve intensely for their pets, and this grief can last a long time. All the vet tech students I interviewed grieved mightily for their pets, and though it had been years since their pets had died, many continued to feel sorrow when they thought about them, especially when they discussed the circumstances of their deaths.

The lack of social support for pet loss can make the journey of grief more difficult than it already is. If someone casually suggests that you're overreacting, you're not likely to confide in them about how terrible you feel. In addition, some of the gestures of support we can count on when we lose a human loved one are absent when we lose a pet. A participant in a pet loss study wrote, "One of the hardest parts is . . . when you feel so alone because there are no gatherings of friends and relatives, no published obituary, no one bringing food, etc. It is as if no one knows how real and deep the loss of the unconditional love can be and so you feel you need to hide or you cannot be true to yourself even after having spent years working on self-esteem and valuing yourself."[13]

Social disenfranchisement also occurs at an institutional level. For example, our religious institutions typically don't offer formal memorial services for animals and may even actively resist offering them, a topic explored at length in *Just an Animal*. Most religiously active people appear to be reluctant to approach their religious leadership or fellow congregants for support after losing a pet. In fact, a cross-cultural study of pet loss in the US and Canada found that, of all the sources of support we might turn to, the least common was clergy (ministers and rabbis).[14]

Similarly, clinical counselors and other mental health practitioners are typically not educated about pet loss and often dismiss a client's grief for their pet as a minor concern. The authors of a US study of pet loss describe an interaction between a woman and her therapist that typifies the lack of understanding among psychological practitioners:

> She had been seeing another therapist in whom she had lost confidence because the therapist had told her, 'The loss of your

friend must be much harder for you than the loss of your dog.' This particular woman had a relationship end with a male friend during the same time she was grieving for her dog. To have assumed that the loss of her friend was more difficult than the loss of her dog negated any value the therapist might have had in this woman's eyes. For this client there was no comparison in magnitude of loss in the two relationships.[15]

Veterinary clinics also lack the support resources that are typically available in human hospitals. When a human loved one dies while in the hospital, family members typically have access to psychologists, social workers, and chaplains. Very few veterinary clinics employ caregivers devoted solely to client support, and research has shown that veterinary workers consider client support among the most stressful aspects of their jobs.[16] Most aren't trained to meet their clients' emotional and spiritual needs, and they also don't have the time because they're often extremely busy. Yet support is sorely needed. A UK study of euthanasia found that pet keepers' level of satisfaction with their veterinary provider depended primarily on the quality of the emotional support they received.[17] More than half of the study participants expressed interest in receiving greater support for their grief from the veterinary team, including personal acknowledgment of the difficulty of pet loss and wishing that veterinary professionals received better training to assist grieving individuals.

The bottom line is that the negative impacts of the cultural issues discussed earlier in this chapter are worse when you lose a pet. If we're expected to recover from our grief quickly and quietly when we lose a human family member, we're expected to recover even faster and with less effort when we lose a pet.

Fortunately, there are encouraging signs that this situation is improving. When I first began my service as a pet chaplain in 2004, there were significantly fewer resources for pet loss than there are at present. Many of these resources are online. Pet memorial websites, social media groups for pet enthusiasts, and pet loss chat rooms have increased in number and popularity over the last twenty years. I'm not convinced that online interactions can replace the support we might receive from people who know us and our pets. But we seek support wherever we can find it, and the popularity of online support resources reflects our need to honor our animals and interact with people who understand what we're going through.

Progress at an institutional level has been slower. Currently, there are only a few educational programs in pet keeping and loss for chaplains, clinical counselors, and social workers. But where there is a need, there is also opportunity, and there is a lot of room for creativity and grassroots work as we consider how best to support each other when we lose our animal companions. With patience and persistence, I believe the day will come when support resources for pet loss are more widely available. This book, along with the other books in the Pet Chaplain Learning Series, was developed to support this transformation.

Improving Our Grief Literacy

It can be difficult to appreciate how powerfully our grief journeys are shaped by the rules of the road in our society—by the things we've learned about grief in our families and communities and absorbed through the media. These messages are subtle and pervasive, and most of us don't tend to question what we've been taught. Because of our social conditioning, we're quick to castigate ourselves when our grief is intense and long-lasting. We rarely afford ourselves time to engage in the slow contemplation that makes healing possible. We've also grown uncomfortable with what we consider negative and unnecessary emotions: sorrow, despair, guilt, and anger, among others. Embarrassed by our feelings and worried that we'll be misunderstood or judged, we struggle to make authentic, meaningful connections with our fellow human beings at a time when we're most in need of support. We often grieve alone, especially when we grieve for animals.

Our unhelpful beliefs about grief, our discomfort with painful emotions, and the chronic shortage of downtime in our society have real consequences in our lives. If we believe we need to move on quickly after our losses or that it's socially unacceptable to share our painful feelings with others, we might avoid engaging with our grief. We also might worry that we're psychologically damaged when the intense pain we suffered after a loss is still with us weeks, months, or years later.

When our grief doesn't work the way we've been taught it should—when our feelings are unpredictable and last a long time—we tend to blame ourselves rather than question the validity of our society's ideas about grief and our collective inability to offer meaningful support to each other. This blame game is played a lot in American culture. We tend to place great responsibility on the individual for everything that goes wrong rather than consider how our society has failed to support us. On a personal level, we struggle to support each other because we haven't been taught how to listen sympathetically to someone who is grieving and demonstrate patience and constancy in the face of intense and long-lasting pain.

Elisabeth Kübler-Ross was a strong advocate for improving people's grief literacy. Although her ideas about grief have fallen out of favor among grief scholars, I have great respect for her astute observations. In the book *On Grief and Grieving*, she asserts that we live in a grief-illiterate culture. "We live in a culture that doesn't know how to grieve," she writes. "We don't know how to experience pain, how to understand its process. We live in a society that wants us to get back to normal as soon as possible. We're expected to go back to work immediately, keep moving, to get on with our lives. But it doesn't work that way."[18]

The point is that the story we tell ourselves about grief is just that—a story. It's not an absolute, unchanging truth, and as a society, we appear to be gradually learning to embrace our grief with grace and dignity. When navigating a pet's end of life, many people are conscientiously focused on giving their animals the best possible life in their final days and a good death as well. We're also learning to give ourselves and others permission to grieve the loss of our animal friends.

In the next two chapters, we'll continue our exploration of grief with a discussion of what's typically described as "grief models." Developed by psychologists who study grief, these models attempt to describe the grief journey and help us understand what we might experience following the loss of a loved one. As we'll see, there's been a sea change in psychological understandings of grief in the last thirty years, and this change is profoundly important to the way we experience grief when we lose a cherished pet.

CHAPTERS 2–5

Discussion Questions

1. Chapter 2 explored five scenarios in which you might feel uncertain or helpless when you lose a pet. Select one or two of these scenarios that resonate with you and tell a brief story about your experience. Describe any thoughts, emotions, and physical sensations you experienced at the time. If you'd like, you can also discuss the loss of a human loved one, wild animals, or a sacred place.

2. Chapter 3 explored common characteristics of grief. Select three you experienced when you lost a pet, a human loved one, a sacred place, or something else, such as the loss of a marriage or a job. Describe how the characteristics you selected emerged for you.

3. Chapter 4 explored the fact that many people struggle with lingering guilt and remorse after losing a pet. Tell a story about a time when you experienced these emotions. Describe what helped you overcome your remorse and what steps you took to forgive yourself.

4. Chapter 4 also explored how guilt is rooted in the powerlessness we feel in the face of death. What are your thoughts on this idea?

5. In chapter 5, we learned that the way we grieve is shaped by cultural norms and by how grief was modeled in our families of origin. Tell a story that demonstrates how you learned about grief in your family of origin. For example, did the adults in your life talk about their feelings when they suffered a loss? How did they respond to your feelings, and how did their responses help or hinder your grief journey?

Continuing Connection

CHAPTER 6

Moving On Versus Staying Connected

Not long after I launched the Pet Chaplain organization in 2004, I visited an animal sanctuary called the Goathouse Refuge, a large acreage in the rolling hills outside Pittsboro, North Carolina. An Italian woman named Siglinda Scarpa owned and managed the rescue, and the occasion was a fundraiser luncheon for the refuge. It was early October when the leaves had begun to change to vivid shades of scarlet, yellow, and orange, and the fall air was crisp and clear. Dozens of peahens chattered and scurried about among the guests, looking for insects. Cats and dogs roamed freely around the property. The entire place felt like a hobbit-style Garden of Eden. I felt overwhelmed by the refuge's eclectic beauty as I made my way to the picnic tables where we would enjoy the delicious lunch Siglinda had prepared.

I took a seat at a large table of about eight people, none of whom I'd met before. People had already started introducing themselves, and I glanced nervously around the table as my turn approached. This was early in my pet ministry, and the title "pet chaplain" was still very new. Yet this seemed like an ideal opportunity to use it.

"Hi, my name is Rob," I said when it was my turn. "I'm a pet chaplain."

I saw a few quizzical looks and heard someone giggle, as if I were joking.

"What's a pet chaplain?" someone called out from the opposite end of the table.

Raising my voice, I gave my best elevator speech. That's when I noticed the older couple seated across from me. The man was looking down at his plate, and the woman was talking softly to him and touching his shoulder. Then he began sobbing, his shoulders shaking as he covered his face with his hands.

The woman glanced at me with a perplexed look. "I'm sorry, but did you say you're a chaplain for pets?" she said.

"No, not for pets," I said. "Though I bless pets. I'm a chaplain to people who've lost a pet."

The man looked up and gazed at me. His bright blue eyes were brimming with tears.

"Are you okay, honey?" his wife asked.

He nodded and looked down again without speaking. Composing herself, the woman said, "I suppose I should explain. Bill is upset about his dog Sammy. He told me the story many years ago."

The woman introduced herself, then shared her husband's story. As a young man, she said, Bill had served in Europe with the American forces during World War II. He was eighteen when he left home, and he made his parents promise to send him regular reports about Sammy until his return. He wrote to them regularly, and they frequently returned letters with stories about his dog.

What they didn't share was the fact that, on the very day Bill left for Europe, Sammy had run into the street and been killed by a car. His parents thought Sammy was looking for Bill, and they feared the truth would devastate him and possibly put him in danger, so they never told him that Sammy had died. Bill didn't find out about Sammy until he returned from the war. He came home unannounced, hoping to surprise his family. But the surprise was his when he rushed through the front door and called for Sammy, but Sammy was nowhere to be found. He found his mother in the kitchen and asked where Sammy was. She hugged him and urged him to sit down, then told him that Sammy was dead. He'd been dead for two years.

"The news crushed him, but he told me he didn't cry," the woman said. "He never spoke about Sammy again. We've been married almost sixty years, and this is the first time I've seen him cry."

I was stunned and at a loss for words. I looked Bill in the eye and told him I was sorry for his loss. He nodded as his wife handed him a tissue.

People like Bill, who lost a pet years ago but never fully grieved the loss, are more numerous than we think. I sometimes imagine thousands, perhaps even millions of people, carrying on with their normal lives, each with a story like Bill's hidden away in their hearts. For countless adults, a pet lost in childhood or young adulthood may never have been fully grieved, or their anguish may have been dismissed or ignored by others. In Bill's generation, stoicism was the rule, and the attitude that pets were possessions or objects that didn't warrant our grief was more prevalent than it is now, though it's still pervasive.

Many of us avoid thinking about our losses, much less talking about them. We minimize our feelings, insisting that we're fine, and we convince ourselves we're fine because we're working a lot, staying busy, and carrying on as if nothing has happened. This "move on" approach to life's challenges may be expedient at times, but it can have long-lasting and sometimes harmful consequences. The truth is, we don't move on easily or quickly after a significant loss. If you don't deal with your grief at some point, that raging river of pain will most likely stay with you. It will simply go underground, and the powerful emotions associated with grief, from guilt and anger to intense sorrow, may reappear in unpredictable ways. For Bill, all it took to reify his grief for his dog Sammy was hearing the words *pet chaplain*.

Grief is not easily set aside, but neither is love. We don't stop loving the people and animals we've lost. We stay connected with our lost loved ones, and these connections can sustain and empower us as we re-create ourselves and our lives.

These two ideas—moving on versus staying connected—represent opposing poles in the understandings of grief that have long dominated the field of psychology and shaped cultural norms about grief in Western society. This chapter explores this dichotomy and provides insight into how our beliefs about grief shape the way we grieve.

Moving On: Detachment Models of Grief

In the early twentieth century, psychiatry pioneer Sigmund Freud described grief as a process through which the griever achieves emotional detachment from an attachment object.[1] According to this idea, the survivor must drain their mental and emotional engine of the psychic energy or libido that was invested in the old relationship and pour that psychic energy into a new attachment object.

This idea eventually became the foundation of what are known as *detachment models of grief*. These models depict love as a form of energy and the human heart as a battery. The thinking goes that we only have so much love at our disposal. When we lose someone we love, we must drain our psychic battery of our attachment to them before we can plug into a new relationship and recharge. If we fail to move on quickly from our losses and reinvest in new relationships, we risk becoming obsessed with the deceased's memory; in turn, we might be unable to move forward and enjoy new relationships. Among psychologists who ascribe to detachment theories of grief, maintaining these attachments is a form of mental illness. As clinical psychologist and grief researcher George Bonanno writes, "According to the traditional theories, the behavior of bereaved people who maintain rather than break bonds with dead loved ones is pathological."[2]

Detachment models of grief have dominated popular conceptions of grief in the West for most of the twentieth century. One of the most well-known is Elisabeth Kübler-Ross's five stages model, which I introduced in chapter 3. The five stages model is so popular, that many of us have internalized the idea that grief follows a predictable trajectory until we're finally able to put the past behind us and move on with our lives. Popular interpretations of this model depict the five stages as linear or progressive. That is, a person is thought to have recovered from grief when they've worked through the stages, fully accepted their loss, moved on with their life, and reinvested their love.

In the decades after the five stages model was introduced in the late 1960s, however, many grief researchers have concluded that the model offers an overly simplistic understanding of a complex emotional experience. One obvious problem is that people often experience emotions not included in the model, such as guilt, remorse, and shame as well as pleasant feelings such as relief and joy. In addition, grief is far more chaotic and unpredictable than the five stages model might lead us to believe. As we saw in the discussion of grief in chapter 3, grief tends to be unpredictable, and it certainly doesn't follow predictable steps or stages.

According to Kübler-Ross, however, the five stages model has been widely misinterpreted. In her final book *On Grief and Grieving*, which she cowrote with David Kessler, she bemoaned the popular belief that the stages imply that grief unfolds predictably and progressively. "The stages have evolved since their introduction, and they have been very misunderstood over the past three decades," she wrote. "They were never meant to help tuck messy emotions into neat packages. . . . The five stages are tools to help us frame and identify what we may be feeling. But they are not stops on some linear timeline in grief. Not everyone experiences all of these emotions, or experiences them in a prescribed order."[3] Kübler-Ross was also concerned that the final stage in her model, acceptance, had been misinterpreted. "Acceptance is often confused with the notion of being all right or okay with what has happened," she wrote. "This is not the case. Most people don't ever feel okay or all right about the loss of a loved one."[4]

Theoretical understandings of grief in the field of psychology have changed substantially since the five stages model was introduced, particularly regarding the notions of acceptance and detachment. This shift is evident in the work of psychologist J. William Worden. In 1976, Worden identified four tasks of mourning and subsequently published his grief model in 1982 in a scholarly book titled *Grief Counseling and Grief Therapy: A Handbook for the Mental Health Practitioner*.[5] In the first edition, the fourth task was worded as "an emotional withdrawal from the deceased person so that this emotional energy can be reinvested in another relationship," a description in keeping with the detachment paradigm.[6] But in the fourth edition of *Grief Counseling*, which was published in 2008, the fourth task had been modified, asserting that grievers need "to find an enduring connection with the deceased in the midst of embarking on a new life."[7]

Another grief expert whose work challenges traditional detachment models is clinical psychologist Alan D. Wolfelt. Wolfelt is the director of the Center for Loss & Life Transition in Fort Collins, Colorado. A researcher and educator, he's written numerous books about grief, and in *Companioning the Bereaved*, he identifies six "needs" of mourning: (1) acknowledging the reality of death; (2) feeling the pain of loss; (3) remembering the person who has died; (4) developing a new identity; (5) searching for meaning; and (6) receiving ongoing support from others.[8] An important aspect of Wolfelt's six needs model is the inclusion of "remembering the person who has died." It's also worth noting that, by using the term *needs* rather than terms like *stages*, *tasks*, or *processes*, Wolfelt avoids the semantic trap of implying that grief has a predictable, linear structure.

Staying Connected: Continuing Bonds

In the field of psychology, the idea that we stay connected with our lost loved ones is known as *continuing bonds*, and it represents a new and influential understanding of grief among grief researchers.[9]

Psychology researchers Dennis Klass, Phyllis Silverman, and Steven Nickman introduced the continuing bonds perspective of grief in 1996 with their groundbreaking book, *Continuing Bonds: New Understandings of Grief*.[10] Written for an academic audience, the book challenged prevailing detachment models by asserting that we do not accept a loved one's death and move on with our lives. Rather, we continue to love them. The loss itself is painful, and the memory of it can remain so for a long time. But people are resilient. As time goes by, our acute feelings of sorrow fade and are replaced by memories of happier times. Contrary to what many of us have been taught, nurturing a healthy emotional connection with our lost loved ones can help us cope.

This understanding reflects what we actually do when we lose a loved one. We stay connected. We keep the flowers fresh on our loved one's grave. We nurture the roses we planted in their honor. We hold onto keepsakes, display their photos in our homes and on social media, and share stories about them with friends and family. We do not detach emotionally from our deceased loved ones, nor do we forget them. We continue to love them for the rest of our lives.

Research bears out what we know in our hearts and witness in our daily lives. Grieving widows and widowers frequently feel the presence of their deceased spouses and regularly interact with them in dreams and conversations. Psychologists refer to such activities as *continuing bond expressions*, and they're very common among people who've lost a human loved one. They're also common among people who've lost a pet. In an online study of people who had lost a dog or cat within a year, participants were asked to reflect on the activities they engaged in following the deaths of their pets.[11] All the participants engaged in activities that helped them maintain a loving connection with their deceased pets. The activities included in the study are listed below, and I've organized them by the percentage of respondents who engaged in each.

- Recalling fond memories (90 percent)

- Saving keepsakes and belongings (79 percent)
- Being influenced by the pet in making everyday decisions and choices (79 percent)
- Talking with the pet (76 percent)
- Having dreams about the pet (76 percent)
- Sensing the pet's presence, such as hearing the pet's sounds or glimpsing them (67 percent)
- Having thoughts of being reunited with the pet (64 percent)
- Creating memorials or shrines or attending special events in tribute to the pet (61 percent)
- Being drawn to or visiting the pet's favorite places (55 percent)
- Living up to the pet's wishes (46 percent)

This is not a definitive list. People find many unique and creative ways to maintain an emotional connection with their lost pets. Some get tattoos, while others preserve a pet's name and avoid using it for another animal. One of the vet tech students I spoke with, a young woman named Anna, said she never uses a pet's name twice. Anna had no keepsakes from her childhood pets—no photographs, collars, or toys—and she also felt she couldn't talk openly about them with her family. For Anna, the most tangible way to honor her pets was to preserve their names.

Another continuing bond expression not addressed directly by the study cited above is when someone receives a sign or message from a deceased pet. This is slightly different than sensing a pet's presence, and it's very common. I also think that sharing stories or reminiscing about a pet with others is a continuing bond expression. When you share a story about your animal with sympathetic listeners, you're calling your pet's memory into the present and strengthening and maintaining your connection with them. You're also enlarging your circle of support.

Finally, I believe that engaging in social, professional, and volunteer activities that honor a pet's legacy is an important continuing bond expression for many people. All the vet tech students I spoke with attributed their interest in veterinary medicine to their experiences with a special pet. Similarly, many people work or volunteer in animal rescue to honor their heart animals. As vet tech student Lillian noted, "My work in rescue is how [my cat Freddie] lives on, and that's because with each life I save, a little piece of his spirit lives on. His life had value. That's the place I eventually came to, and I found peace in that." I refer to this phenomenon as *generativity*, which involves honoring the life of a loved one through one's work and volunteer activities or by conscientiously paying the love forward.[12] Generativity is one of the most important concepts that emerged in my study of the vet tech students, and I'll return to this idea in chapter 9.

Help or Hindrance?

Is the maintenance of continuing bonds with a pet helpful or harmful when we're grieving? Psychologists who subscribe to detachment theories typically criticize the concept of continuing bonds. They argue that the comfort we find in memories of our lost loved ones is an illusion and, ultimately, a barrier to fully accepting our losses and recovering from our grief. In contrast, proponents assert that continuing bonds represent a healthy response to loss and can aid in coping.

Psychologist George Bonanno advocates for the continuing bonds understanding of grief. In 2009, his book *The Other Side of Sadness: What the New Science of Bereavement Tells Us About Life After Loss* brought this new understanding of grief to a popular audience. Bonnano's research with widows and widowers shows that those who could connect with happy memories of the deceased fared better than those who could not. "People who are able to deal with a loved one's death, and who are able to accept the finality of the loss, are also able to find comfort in memories of that [loved one]," writes Bonanno. "They know their loved one is gone, but when they think and talk about the deceased, they find that they haven't lost everything. The relationship is not completely gone. They can still call to mind and find joy in the positive shared experiences. It is as if some part of the relationship is still alive."[13]

My own research into pet loss supports Bonanno's position. In fact, the continuing bonds understanding of grief was one of the primary concerns of my doctoral research study among the vet tech students I interviewed.[14] All the students maintained continuing bonds with their deceased pets, and all appeared to benefit from these connections. Their stories, ten of which are included in *Heart Animals*, the first book in the learning series, demonstrate that their pets continued to be a powerful presence in their lives. They expressed sadness or sometimes cried when talking about their animals' deaths, but they also took comfort in their memories of the happy times they'd shared. As Kelly said, "I still love all my old pets, even the ones that I wasn't super attached to. I still love them like crazy. Whenever I talk about the pets I've lost, I talk about them as if they were still alive. Because in some ways they are. They're all still with me, in my heart."

I also discovered that the love the students felt for their pets did not appear to diminish with time. Frank had lost his cat Muppet eight years prior to our interview but still loved her as much as he did when she was still alive. "I can still feel Muppet rub up against my leg," Frank told me. "I can actually *feel* her. If the cat I have now jumps up in my lap, I think of how Muppet would stretch out and wrap her limbs around my legs. There are a lot of things that spark those memories, those sensations. I constantly see her. I don't even have to close my eyes, and I can see her. Even though she's gone, she's still with me all the time in heart and spirit. She's just part of my life. I can still feel the love."

In my experience, most pet keepers appear to benefit from continuing bonds with their deceased pets. Many build shrines in their homes that are filled with pictures and keepsakes of their pet. Some plant a tree in their pet's honor; hold a memorial with family and friends; write a eulogy or an online dedication; and otherwise hold tight to their joyful memories. The point is to find what works for you. There are many ways to maintain a healing connection with a deceased pet, and all can potentially help you cope with your loss.

As comforting and beneficial as maintaining a continuing bond with a deceased pet may be, I would be remiss to imply that this experience is all joy and light. In the study of continuing bonds among pet keepers mentioned earlier in this chapter, the authors concluded that their findings "supported both the adaptive nature of continuing bonds as well as their distressing nature."[15]

So how might a continuing bond be more distressing than comforting? In my experience, the more recent your loss, the more difficult it might be to find comfort in things that remind you of your pet. A man who participated in the continuing bonds study remarked, "It is really distressing because . . . oh, just everything . . . going to the market, not having him there, running errands. . . . I can't go to the beach yet, but going to the park, even walking down the street, was hard. I think about him all the time, and everything is a memory. And it's distressing because he's not there. So no, it's not good happy. It's good happy memories but it's upsetting."[16]

The tension between happy memories and dreaded reminders of a deceased pet tends to ease with time. In fact, you might discover that the very things that once made you painfully aware of your animal's absence eventually inspire good feelings. This was my friend Bryan's experience after he lost his dog, Ringo. "At first, I couldn't look at his pictures," Bryan said. "It was too painful. But now I can enjoy the memories. I can tell stories about him and laugh. I can think fondly of him." Among the vet tech students I interviewed, it had been an average of nine years since they'd lost their pets. Each had had at least a year to engage with their grief before the interview, so it's not surprising that all drew comfort from their continuing bonds and delighted in sharing stories about their animals. If I'd talked with them just after their losses,

I expect some would have reported, like Bryan, that looking at their pet's pictures was painful.

Another situation that can make reminders of your pet distressing is if their death was sudden, violent, or painful. Elaine, whose story about her dog Harvey appears in chapter 3, found that thinking about him after his death inevitably transported her to the horrible moment when she discovered his lifeless body. She said that the night before his death, they had sat on the couch together and shared some popcorn, a happy ritual they had enjoyed many times. But after Harvey's death, even the smell of popcorn triggered a painful flashback for Elaine. "I still find it very hard to talk about Harvey and about what happened," she said. "My heart is full of him because I loved him so much. And sometimes I'll kind of allude to him, but it's a very sore spot in my heart, because if I think or talk about him, it all comes back. I think about how he must have suffered, and that's a memory that haunts me sometimes." As Bonanno observes, "[some] bereaved people, those who are more debilitated by loss, find it harder to hold onto positive memories, as if they can no longer find the [loved one] they lost, as if the memories are hidden from them. The pain of grief, it seems, can block all memories of the good."[17]

If you've recently lost a pet and feel so overwhelmed with sorrow that you're unable to comfortably think about them or engage in activities that remind you of them, my recommendation is to give yourself time to heal. If looking at your pet's possessions or photos is distressing, consider storing them out of sight until you're ready to go through them. It's also important to pay attention to the emotions that arise when you think about your pet. As we saw in chapter 4, guilt and remorse are difficult to resolve, especially when avenues to forgiveness seem absent or blocked. You might feel trapped in an endless cycle of self-recrimination for your pet's death. Being overwhelmed by these distressing feelings can make it difficult to connect with your positive memories and once again experience the love and happiness you enjoyed in your pet's company.

Extraordinary Experiences

Of the ten continuing bond expressions listed earlier in this chapter, there's one I'd like to discuss in greater detail: sensing a deceased pet's presence. Some people report hearing their pet's sounds or glimpsing them from the corner of their eye. Others say they felt their pet jump up on their bed at night. A similar phenomenon is when you believe your pet has sent you a sign or message from the "other side." You might perceive these messages as being transmitted through other animals or natural phenomena, such as a butterfly that swoops down and lights upon your hand as you kneel next to your pet's grave or a beautiful rainbow that suddenly appears just as thoughts of your animal enter your mind.

I'd like to share a few stories that speak to this phenomenon and how our interpretation of these events can either help or hinder our grief journeys. A few years ago, a friend of mine contacted me on behalf of an acquaintance. She told me that this acquaintance had been out of town and left her dog in the care of a neighbor, but the dog got out of the house and was killed by a car. On numerous occasions following her dog's death, the woman thought she heard him scratching at the back door to be let in, but when she went to the door, nothing was there. These episodes were very distressing for her. My friend asked if I believed the dog's spirit was lingering on Earth, waiting for assistance to move on, or perhaps the dog was trying to contact the woman to let her know that he was fine.

I told my friend that such incidents are common, and I acknowledged that they can be distressing. I also assured her that such experiences would most likely diminish within a few months. If I had been working directly with the woman whose dog had been hit and killed by a car, I would have asked a few open-ended questions to gauge her feelings about the tragic circumstances of her dog's death. I would encourage her to consider ways she might forgive herself and the neighbor who was caring for her dog. My concern is that her interpretation of this extraordinary experience—that her dog's spirit was lingering and unable to "move on"—was possibly wrapped up with her guilt and the tragic circumstances of her dog's death.

Notably, the friend who'd contacted me also mentioned she'd had a personal experience of a visitation from her deceased service dog. About a week after he was euthanized, she was lying down for a nap one afternoon, and she called out to him as was her habit. She felt him jump up on the bed and curl up against the small of her back, just as he did when he was still living. For her, the experience was a comforting affirmation that her dog was happy and that he would always be with her.

My friend Linda Moore, an Episcopal priest who graduated from my veterinary chaplaincy course, also had an extraordinary experience after losing her dog, Maggie, a yellow Labrador retriever. Maggie had fought a long battle against cancer and underwent many painful procedures, and Linda felt guilty for putting her beloved dog through it all only to lose her in the end. When Maggie died, Linda said she "grieved hard, praying every day for a sign that she was OK somewhere and that she loved me still." Linda also said that for months she couldn't find the strength to vacuum the back seat of her car, which was still covered in Maggie's yellow fur. Six months after Maggie's death, she decided it was time to clean things up, so she went to a car wash:

> I stopped at the car wash and began to vacuum the back seat of my car. I was sobbing. It felt like I was losing another part of Maggie. There were no other cars there, no other people. As I was leaning into my car, I felt a gentle nudge on my leg, just like Maggie used to nudge me. I turned around, and there was a yellow lab standing there smiling at me. I have to admit, I felt that I might be hallucinating. But no, the dog was real. He was a beauty. I heard someone call for him, and it turned out there was an apartment behind the car wash that I had no idea was there. I'd been to that car wash many times before

and many times since. But I've only seen this wonderful yellow lab once. I was reassured then that Maggie still watches over her earthly mama. I believe that Maggie and God, my great Mother, brought this dog to me. It was so amazing to me, so healing.

Linda's unexpected encounter with the yellow lab at the car wash was a "shimmering moment"—a deeply meaningful experience that strengthened her spiritual connection with her beloved Maggie.[18] The phrase *shimmering moment* was coined by therapist Pamela A. Hays to describe those memorable experiences that become touchpoints we return to repeatedly throughout our lives. I introduced this concept in a discussion of human spirituality in *Heart Animals*, the first book in the learning series. Shimmering moments can feel redeeming, like cosmic or divine affirmations. They sometimes lead to a spiritual awakening because they compel us to pause and reflect on life's greater meaning and potentially arrive at insights that help us live more fully and with a greater sense of purpose.

The extraordinary experiences I've described here can't be easily explained by the scientific laws or principles we currently understand, so they're generally considered pseudoscientific. But in the realm of spirituality, such experiences brim with meaning. I encourage you to embrace these rare moments with wonder and curiosity and to give careful thought to how they make you feel and the meanings they hold for you.

Embracing New Understandings of Grief

In this chapter, we've explored two psychological understandings of grief that offer very different perspectives about how we manage our feelings of attachment to a deceased loved one. We began with a review of traditional detachment models of grief, which hold that we must sever our emotional attachments to recover from our grief and seek out new relationships. In contrast, the continuing bonds understanding of grief holds that these connections can comfort the bereaved and aid with coping. This perspective is gaining acceptance among grief researchers and represents a profound shift in psychological understandings of this common human experience.

Unfortunately, it can take a long time for ideas that have gained traction in academia to trickle into the public consciousness. As previously noted, most grief researchers assert that the five stages model depicts the grieving experience too narrowly. Despite these challenges, however, the five stages model continues to dominate online discussions of grief. One survey found that more than 60 percent of websites that talk about grief uncritically promote the five stages model and 75 percent depict grief as something that occurs in stages, although these websites don't reference the model directly.[19] Some grief experts believe that the continued promotion of the five stages model may actually be harmful to the unsuspecting public. As noted in an article on the website *Psychology Today*, "The unfortunate side effect of our society's erroneous but firm belief in the five stages is that many people wind up criticizing themselves for 'not doing grief right.'"[20]

Most of us have been socially conditioned to think we need to move on quickly from our losses. Indeed, the five stages model is so popular that most people are familiar with it and some can name all the stages. I've sometimes asked attendees of my pet loss support group what they know about grief. Almost all name the five stages, but when I mention the continuing bonds understanding of grief, no one has ever heard of it. Ironically, almost every person can share a photo of a memorial or shrine they've created to honor their lost pets.

I can only guess at the reasons that detachment models of grief like the five stages continue to be widespread in our society. One possibility is that stepwise models of grief offer simple, straightforward explanations for a complex phenomenon. Facing an unknown future without our pets can be frightening, so the more we can predict what might happen and what we'll experience, the better we tend to feel. In this way, the five stages and similar detachment models serve as a roadmap for the chaotic and disorienting grief journey. Because they break grief down into manageable stages, tasks, or steps, they appear to offer us an orderly way to make sense of our sorrow and find relief quickly. As helpful as this depiction of grief might seem, it's also inaccurate and, as we've seen, it might even do us more harm than good.

The continuing bonds understanding of grief provides a new way of thinking and talking about the death of a loved one and life after loss. It's based on the principle that love is an unlimited resource that survives death. Indeed, it's probably more accurate to refer to continuing bonds simply as continuing love. We never stop loving the pets we've lost, and the creative ways we find to express and maintain this love can help us cope with our grief. In other words, the loss does not change the love; the love transforms the loss. When you embrace this simple wisdom, you might discover that the love you still feel for the pets you've lost can guide you to peace and healing.

CHAPTER 7

Coping with Loss

I met Kim McCool when she participated in my veterinary chaplaincy course. She enrolled after doing some spiritual direction work at her church and said that animals had emerged as an important focus for her. A retired corporate project manager, she had plans to launch a pet ministry at her church.

Kim was a great student: highly motivated, well-spoken, sensitive and kind to her fellow students, and passionate about animals. During the course, Kim shared that she was hit especially hard by the loss of her dog Holly, a toy schnauzer. Holly was born in a puppy mill and suffered from many health problems throughout her short life. She died when she was only six years old after a sudden, brief illness. Kim was devastated.

"Holly was the sweetest, most even-tempered little thing you'd ever hope to meet," Kim said. "Because of her health problems, I felt the need to be more attentive, more protective of her than with other pets, which led to me being more in tune and in sync with her needs, her feelings, and her pain. I also felt a strong spiritual connection with Holly, and because of that connection, her death hit me harder than any other pet I'd ever owned. I've grieved for all my pets, but the grief

I felt for Holly was the longest in duration, the deepest, most shattering experience I've ever gone through."

Every day for a month after Holly died, Kim recorded her thoughts and feelings in a journal. She found it was the only way she could manage her grief. Below are some excerpts. It's a moving account of the intense pain Kim endured and all the reminders of Holly's absence that punctuated her days, evoking bittersweet memories and an intense longing to have Holly back in her life.

September 7: Dearest Holly—two days without you. I can't believe you are gone. I find myself caught between continual tears and the slight hope I will hear your little bell tinkling as you trot around the corner to me. I've lost animals before, and they were all difficult to say goodbye to, but your passing is different somehow. I feel like there is a giant hole in my heart, and what remains of my heart has shattered into a million pieces.

September 10: Five days without you. Last night was tough. Dean and I went to a birthday party, and people were asking about you. I couldn't say the words. I couldn't bring myself to tell them you were gone. I was afraid I would burst into tears. I simply said you were doing well. Dean knew how difficult it was for me and hugged my shoulder.

September 11: This morning, I was putting something away in the pantry and noticed the rubber mat I used to put in the bottom of the sink when you got your bath. You didn't care too much for baths, but you knew there was a treat waiting when I put you on the counter to dry you off. I'd put you down on the floor, and you'd race around the house like greased lightning. Dean and I would laugh so! But you'd get so cold. You'd shiver so much after your run. To keep you warm, I'd put some towels in the dryer before we started our bath so they would be toasty warm. I'd wrap you in one and hold you until it cooled, then get another toasty warm one and hold you until you'd fall asleep. I guess that's why I started calling you My Little Toaster. I miss you!

September 12: A week without you. I thought I heard your voice waking me up this morning—you know, that "urrr" sound you would make. I keep your collar next to my side of the bed now. I had asked Dean to take the bell and tags off, but then I asked him to put them back on. A friend called yesterday to chat and asked me if we would be getting another dog. I told her no, not now. You are not replaceable.

As Kim discovered, it's often the simple things we miss most when our pets are no longer with us. You might sorely miss the signs of your animal's reliable presence in your daily life: the sound of their voice, the scuffle of their feet on the floor, the soft touch of their fur, their quirks and routines, and the joyful, loving energy they brought to your life. You might feel as if a gaping hole has opened not only in your heart but also in every room of your home and every second of your day. For many of us, our pets *are* home—our emotional and spiritual centers—and when they're gone, the dwelling we inhabit can feel cold and foreign. You might feel your pet's absence especially hard when you return home after a long day at work or school and they're no longer there to greet you. Rather than being restful, such quiet can feel eerie and terribly lonely.

I've heard this unsettling quiet referred to as the "loudest silence," and it's a phenomenon many people who've attended my pet loss support group remark upon. One woman noticed how quiet her and her husband's home became when the last of their four dogs died. "We were used to hearing the dogs running around or grooming themselves or barking and licking," she said. "I didn't realize how quiet it would be without them there. It got real quiet and not in a good way." Similarly, a young man who'd recently lost his dog described how completely the atmosphere in his home changed. "We had a baby in the house," he said. "It's weird to describe the house as being quiet after our dog passed away, especially when you've got a two-and-a-half-year-old running around screaming. But the house was really quiet. We didn't have our dog to take care of anymore. We both really missed those routines."

The changes you experience in your daily routines after losing a pet can be one of the most difficult aspects of the grief journey. Deciding what to do with your pet's possessions, tending to the grief of other pets, and deciding if and when to get another pet are also challenging. Yet there are many practical things you can do to fill the silence and cope with the ever-present reminders of your pet's physical absence. This can be as simple as adjusting your daily routines and as elaborate as creating a shrine for your pet or gathering friends and family for a memorial. Such activities will help you survive your grief, especially soon after a loss. But in the long run, they can also help you process your feelings and begin to make sense of your loss.

This chapter explores some of the difficult decisions you might need to make soon after a loss. It also reviews a variety of coping strategies that can help you make it through your day and begin to discover the deeper meanings hidden in your grief.

Adjusting Your Daily Routines

The routines associated with caring for a pet—from feeding and grooming to exercising and playing or cuddling—provide the framework for the daily activities of many devoted pet keepers. Your schedule might be built around your pet's needs. When you lose them, you're likely to face constant reminders of their absence.

Adjusting to life without your pet can be particularly challenging if you've cared for an old or ill animal for a long time. While you might miss your pet and the intimacy you shared, you might also miss being needed. The cycle of caregiving has been broken, and your identity as a caregiver has been lost. You might struggle to find a new sense of purpose and wonder how to fill the many empty hours previously devoted to caregiving. In this scenario, losing your pet is a double loss: the loss of your pet *and* your sense of self as a caregiver.

People respond differently to their pet's absence. Many are driven by the need to get a little relief from the shock and acute grief that comes in death's wake. Some find it helpful to stick with the routines associated with their pet, at least for a little while. A young woman who came to my pet loss support group mentioned how much she missed having her dog around, even though he slept most of the time in his final weeks. She was in the habit of walking her dog every night before bed, and she missed that routine so much that she kept taking those walks after her dog passed. "I was so conditioned to walking him at night that, after he passed away, I had to still go walk him," she recalled. "I took the empty leash, and I grabbed a poopy bag on the way out the door, and I walked down the street, because that is what I'd done for ten years. I needed some sense of normalcy. I needed what was. I missed the routine."

In contrast, you might find it helpful to change your routines and avoid situations that remind you of your pet, at least temporarily. Maybe you continue to take walks the way you used to, but you change your route. Or maybe instead of having your first cup of coffee in the living room, where your cat used to curl up on your lap, you move to the kitchen. I typically encourage people to try different things and see what helps them get through the day. Adjusting your routines won't necessarily lessen your pain, but it can at least make life more tolerable.

Dealing with Your Pet's Possessions

Dealing with a pet's possessions is another thorny issue. People respond to this challenge in different ways. Perhaps you can't bear to part with your pet's toys, bedding, and other keepsakes because such reminders bring up so many precious memories. You might consider using some of these possessions to create a memorial or shrine to your pet in your home. On the other hand, you might find it too painful to keep your pet's things around because you feel your pet's absence more acutely when you see them. You might be tempted to clear out all these reminders to avoid or distract yourself from your sorrow. Though understandable, if you eliminate all reminders of your pet's absence now, you might come to regret that decision down the road.

I generally encourage people who've recently lost a pet to avoid doing anything they can't easily undo. It's better to wait until your life has stabilized a bit before making any big decisions about your pet's possessions or other physical reminders of them. Instead, consider stowing them in a keepsake box you can go through later once your most intense grief has begun to ease.

When Other Animals in Your Household Grieve

If you keep multiple pets, your surviving animals may grieve the loss of their friend. Although it's not clear whether all animals experience grief, research shows that dogs and cats—like other highly social species such as crows, elephants, dolphins, and primates—exhibit signs of grief when a member of their social group dies.

According to a grief handout from the veterinary school at Ohio State University, surviving animals may exhibit a variety of behavioral and emotional changes following the death of another pet, noting that these animals "may cling to their human family members, be more reactive to stimuli, appear anxious or depressed, and demonstrate a loss of interest in playing, sleeping, or eating. Changes in lifestyle can be stressful on pets, and some may show signs of separation anxiety. This may include panting, pacing, whining, drooling, howling, barking, and not eating treats when left alone."[1] A New Zealand study of cats and dogs who had lost an animal in their household supports these observations. Three-quarters of study participants said their dogs and cats demanded more attention from them after an animal companion died, and they also spent time in the missing animal's favorite places.

About a third of dogs ate less food less quickly than before, and they also slept more, while cats tended to become highly vocal.[2] Conflicts may also arise between pets when one of their pack members is lost, especially if that animal was the leader. A new pecking order has to be established, which can be a stressful process.

Another troubling behavior is when an animal wanders around your home in search of their lost companion. They may engage in the same searching behavior when a human family member is lost. I once heard a story about a woman whose husband had died in the hospital. The couple's dog wandered from room to room, crying and whining, but no matter what she did, the dog was inconsolable. The woman finally reached out to the funeral director who was preparing her husband's body for interment and arranged to have his body temporarily returned to her home. Her dog became calm and ceased crying and whining once she had a chance to see and smell the man's body.

Giving animals the opportunity to see and smell a deceased pet's body appears to help them cope better. If your pet was euthanized at your veterinary clinic, it might be a good idea to bring their body home so your other animals can see and smell it. In-home euthanasia also gives surviving pets a chance to interact with their companion's body. According to veterinarian Dr. Christine Scott, an in-home euthanasia specialist, "Animals are far more intuitive about each other than people realize, and being present [at a euthanasia] can help their grieving process."

So how should you respond to distressing changes in the behavior of your surviving pets? In my view, one of the best things you can do is to maintain your daily routines as much as possible. Animals are very attuned to their environment and to you and your family members, so any dramatic changes in your eating, exercising, playing, and sleeping habits may exacerbate their stress. As noted earlier, you might feel inclined to change some of your routines, especially those that remind you of your lost pet. But maintaining a predictable daily schedule can also be helpful for you and your surviving animals since these activities provide structure at a time when familiar routines have been disrupted.

You might also be tempted to try to hide your grief from your other pets. Friends, professional caregivers, and websites or books about pet loss might even advise you to do so. On a web page concerning grief among surviving pets published by VCA animal hospitals, which maintains clinics throughout the US, pet keepers who've lost a pet are encouraged to "express their grief privately" and avoid showing their feelings in front of their surviving animals. "It's instinctive to lean on your pet for comfort as you process your own grief, but try not to become too emotional in front of your pet," the article advises. "Your pet is sensitive to your feelings, and your grief may add to his distress. It's fine to allow your pet to snuggle, but try to be aware of his response to your emotions. Talk to your pet in an upbeat voice even when you are sad."[3]

We all want to be good caregivers for our animals, yet I believe it's inadvisable to regularly suppress your grief. Not only is this unhealthy, but it probably won't work. Your surviving pets will most likely know that something is troubling you, even if you manage to feign happiness. They're very sensitive to our emotions, which is one of the qualities we value most about them. As one pet keeper observed, "I don't even have to cry. My dog just knows. Even when I think I'm doing a good job of being stoic and turning my face into a neutral, emotionless mask, [my dog] has the amazing ability to sense my inner turmoil, and he'll run over to me, rest his head and his paw on my knee to get my attention, . . . [and] once I acknowledge him, he'll lean in, cover my face with licks, and snuggle up to me."[4]

In my view, it's best to grieve openly with all your family members—both human and animal—when a pet is lost. Let your pets feel their feelings and express them in their unique way, and you should strive to do the same. Comfort and support each other. Receive your animals' love and concern and return it to them in equal measure.

Getting Another Pet

Another difficult question you might face after losing a pet is when to bring another animal into your life, assuming you don't have other animals already. The way people respond to this decision varies greatly. I've heard many stories about animals who arrived in someone's life soon after they'd lost their pet. Perhaps a stray cat showed up at your door, or you were randomly contacted a day after your dog was euthanized by someone seeking a home for a puppy they could no longer care for. Some people interpret the incidental arrival of a new pet as a cosmic affirmation—one of those shimmering moments I mentioned earlier—or a gift or message from their deceased animal.

I've also met people for whom adopting a new pet soon after losing another seems like a good option. The new animal helps them cope with their grief, and they simply like having a pet around to care for. These individuals seem able to simultaneously open their hearts to a new animal while still honoring their memories of the pet who died. My friends Alan and Sandra Mixon are among those pet keepers who were eager to welcome a new pet into their lives soon after they lost their dog Bella, a feisty terrier mix who weighed thirteen pounds and had only three teeth. Bella had belonged to Sandra's mother. When her mother passed, Sandra adopted Bella, even though she and Alan had never kept a pet before. Bella changed their lives. They both fell in love with her, and she was always with them. Sandra is confined to a wheelchair, and Bella typically rode around on Sandra's lap throughout the day. The couple works at my local community center, which Karen and I visit every Wednesday night for a ballroom dance event that we help coordinate. When Bella passed unexpectedly, Alan and Sandra were distraught. We held a small memorial event in Bella's honor at one of the Wednesday night dances, and the couple created a shrine of pictures and other mementos in their living room. Within two weeks, the couple welcomed another dog into their lives when they adopted an older Yorkie mix from a local rescue organization. They promptly named their new girl Stella.

"I just really missed having Bella around, cuddling with her and getting kisses from her," Sandra said. "Stella is a lot different than Bella, and I will always love Bella, but it has helped me a lot to have Stella around. And I feel good about adopting Stella because she was an older dog, and she was in rough shape. We're all doing better now that we have Stella to love on."

Yet the decision to welcome a new pet into our lives is never straightforward. Making a big decision like this—or any other significant change to your life—when your grief is fresh can be risky. It's important to consider your options and weigh the pros and cons of bringing a new animal into your life before taking the plunge. If you've recently lost a pet and are considering getting another, I encourage you to reflect carefully on whether you've given yourself enough time to process your grief for the loss of your animal. Is it possible that you're using a new pet to fill your home's intolerable emptiness and soothe your woundedness?

If asked, I usually encourage pet keepers to wait at least a year after a pet's death before bringing a new animal into their lives. This gives you an opportunity to mark important anniversaries in the life you shared with your animal, such as birthdays and holidays. It also gives you time to grieve for your pet and move farther along on your grief journey before welcoming a new animal into your home.

Coping Strategies

When you're caught in the throes of intense grief, staying fully present to the swirling cloud of painful thoughts, emotions, and physical sensations that have taken over your life can be intolerable. Humans have a strong need to feel like we're moving forward in some way, that we're taking action and gaining control over our lives. To compensate for our pain and our need for agency, we tend to spend a lot of time ruminating on the past, particularly about the events and decisions that culminated in a pet's death. Such thinking can also focus on the future. You might worry about your other pets and think through everything you'll need to do to avoid the same outcome with a different animal. You also might worry that your friends and coworkers will notice that you're feeling down or that you'll burst into tears when you pass the pet food aisle at the grocery store. When your grief is intense, anything—the past or the future—may seem better than now. Because this moment is agonizing.

This is why coping strategies are so important. The activities listed below can help free you from obsessive thoughts about the past and future, at least temporarily. They might also give you some agency at a time when you're feeling completely helpless and out of control. Some of these activities will encourage you to process your feelings and be present with your emotions. Holding a memorial for your animal, creating a daily gratitude list, engaging in creative work, and sharing your story with others are particularly suitable for this purpose.

- Practice good self-care
- Prepare in advance for your pet's death
- Make a donation or volunteer
- Save keepsakes and make a shrine or dedication
- Hold a memorial for your pet
- Engage in spiritual or religious practices
- Keep a daily gratitude list
- Engage in creative work
- Share your story with others

We'll review these strategies in greater detail in the remainder of this chapter. When reading this material, give some thought to your grieving style. Grief researchers have identified two primary grieving styles.[5] *Instrumental* grievers tend to experience their grief cognitively and physically, and they may cope in behavioral ways, for example, by building something to memorialize their deceased pet. In contrast, *intuitive* grievers tend to withdraw from normal activity and build a protective shell around themselves in which they can tend to their wounds. Intuitive grievers may gravitate toward activities such as journaling or other creative work that encourages the contemplation and expression of thoughts and feelings. The instrumental versus intuitive styles of grieving fall on a continuum, so many people possess aspects of both.

Before we begin, I'd like to offer a gentle reminder that the activities described here are not intended to cure your grief. If your grief is intense, you might be frustrated and disheartened if you throw yourself into these activities and see no appreciable change in your suffering. You might feel like you're simply going through the motions, but your heart is still broken. Yet I have faith that, with time and perseverance, you'll begin to enjoy more good days than bad as you engage with some or all these activities.

Practice good self-care

No matter where you are on your grief journey, it's essential to practice good self-care, and this is especially important soon after a loss when your grief is most intense and you're struggling to function in basic ways. At a minimum, drink plenty of fluids, eat nutritious meals, and get as much rest as possible. Simplify meals by grazing throughout the day or by enlisting friends and family to help prepare food. Exercise can be particularly helpful for relieving stress, assuming your overall health is good.

It may also be helpful to occasionally take a break from grief. A get-together with friends or family, an outing to a movie, concert, or sporting event, picking up a new hobby or engaging in an old one, or otherwise temporarily setting your grief aside may help you get through those days when the pain of your pet's absence permeates every moment. As I've said, grief needs to be attended to, but you don't have to be a slave to it, and taking breaks can help you enjoy a comforting sense of normalcy.

If you're really struggling to function, talk to your doctor about medications to temporarily manage your anxiety and sadness. I hesitate to offer this last suggestion because, as noted earlier, grief is often medicalized in our society, and health-care professionals may be quick to prescribe medications for grief. Nonetheless, some people find it impossible to carry on with their normal lives without some pharmaceuticals to help them better manage their grief and the demands of work, school, and family life.

Prepare in advance for your pet's death

We generally think of coping as something we do after a loss, but there is a great deal we can do to prepare for a pet's death. I consider preplanning an important coping strategy because it can help you navigate your animal's end of life with greater confidence and agency. It can also make your grief following their death easier to manage.

When it comes to preplanning, most people think of the advance directives we typically complete for ourselves or a human loved one. End-of-life (EOL) planning for pets is growing in popularity because it offers so many benefits. I recommend consulting your veterinarian to create an EOL document. If you take time now to make decisions about euthanasia, rituals of passage, after-death body care, and other important questions, you won't be burdened by worries that you made important decisions in a rush or when you weren't able to think through them carefully.

Preplanning can also include taking extra good care of your animal in their final days. Preparing in advance for your pet's death benefits you and your animal. Some people create bucket lists for their animals and engage in as many of their animals' favorite activities as possible, given their physical capabilities. Others make a point of spending extra time with their animal and giving them extra attention.

People who've adopted this mindset are finding many creative ways to ensure that their animal's final days are the best they can possibly be.

The testimony of Cindi Rodriguez, who studied veterinary chaplaincy with me, offers insight into the advantages of preparing well in advance for a pet's death. When her dog Mercedes's health began to decline, Cindi focused on giving her the best life possible. She took her off some medications that were sapping Mercedes's energy and practiced massage and Reiki instead. "If she had one good week, I was happy," Cindi said. "I would rather give her one more of her best weeks than give me another month of time with her when she wasn't feeling like herself. I wanted her to live her best life. I spent those months of Mercedes's failing health reflecting and meditating with her. I never thought that the bond we shared for thirteen years could grow even stronger, but it did. We had special music we listened to and special times and touches. We had a way of communicating that only we knew."

Then the day arrived that Cindi knew Mercedes was dying. "I felt it in her skin," Cindi said. "I mean, I knew this dog. I knew her every touch, and her skin was not right. . . . When the day came that she was slipping away, we went to the veterinarian for her euthanasia. We listened to our music and held our special touch. Our hearts and souls connected. She knew my heart was breaking to lose her presence, but it was time, and I stayed strong for her as she drifted away. She went peacefully. And I was peaceful. I don't think I shed a single tear because I'd learned how to be calm and strong for her."

When she reflected on Mercedes's death, Cindi was thankful to have chosen the path she did. "I'd lost dogs where I was a hysterical mess," Cindi said. "I couldn't let go of the dog. I was solving problems all the time. But then you realize—what good did that do for the dog? I came to realize that it's not about me and what I need. It always has to be about what's best for the animal."

Cindi's story is a good reminder of what's possible when we find the courage to face death head-on and make the best of the cards we've been dealt. Though it broke her heart to lose Mercedes, she transformed what could have been an agonizing experience into something beautiful. And because she found the courage to respond to Mercedes's failing health so lovingly, Cindi was able to look back on the experience with pride rather than remorse. She knew she'd made the right decisions for Mercedes, which helped strengthen the bond she continued to feel for her after she was gone. It also made her grief journey easier to manage.

Make a donation or volunteer

A great way to honor a deceased pet is to make a donation or volunteer with an organization whose mission aligns with your personal values, such as an animal rescue organization. Volunteering can also be helpful because it empowers you to take action and do good in the world in your pet's name. Volunteering in a rescue shelter, for example, will encourage you to step out of your grief and make meaningful connections with others who share your love of animals. My friend Mary DeRosa, who studied veterinary chaplaincy with me, credits her rescue work with helping her manage her grief after she lost her cat Linus. "I remember feeling that I needed to do something to deal with the grief," Mary said. "I don't know why I thought about animal rescue, but I guess I thought that helping other people or helping the animals would help me feel better. And it did. My rescue work helped me get out of my head."

Save keepsakes and make a shrine or dedication

Keepsakes, shrines, and dedications or tributes represent physical vessels for our continuing bonds with deceased pets. Many people display photos or painted portraits of their pet along with their pet's collar or favorite toy and their urn. Artists who specialize in animal portraits and pet figurines abound. Ceramic paw prints, locks of hair, pendants or other glass objects made from a pet's ashes, key chains that feature a pet's photo, and other items are all continuing bond expressions that can be an ongoing source of comfort. Some people get a tattoo of their pet's paw print or another image that reminds them of their pet. If your pet is interred in your yard or at a pet cemetery, you might wish to decorate their burial site with a gravestone or plaque, flowers, and other meaningful items. Some people plant a tree or other favorite perennial in their pet's honor or purchase a plaque or brick at a local rescue organization as a dedication to their pet. Such remembrances are long-lasting and provide tangible objects you can treasure and physical places you can visit for years to come. Be creative and find what works for you.

Hold a memorial service for your pet
Holding a memorial service for your pet is a great way to grieve, connect with others, and honor your pet's memory. Like other creative endeavors, organizing a memorial that includes personally meaningful reflections, poems, or sacred writings is a great way to explore your feelings, celebrate your animal's unique qualities and gifts, and articulate what they mean to you.

A memorial for your pet doesn't have to be elaborate to be deeply meaningful. The simple act of gathering loved ones to look at pictures, share stories, and discuss why that animal was loved can help you connect with others when you may feel isolated. Collective mourning rituals are powerfully healing because they affirm the value of what has been lost. By honoring your pet as a valued member of your family and sharing those sentiments with the people in your life, you might discover that your community lightens the heavy burden of your grief. Some people hold a memorial for their animal at the time of their death or soon after. Others need more time to think about what they want to say. There's no rush. Do what feels right to you.

Engage in spiritual or religious practices
Our spiritual or religious beliefs and practices can offer comfort and guidance when we've lost a loved one. Notably, of all the ways we might

maintain a connection with our deceased pets, the belief that we will be reunited in the afterlife is among the most comforting. A study of US pet keepers found that, of all the options available for memorializing pets, such as displaying a photo or keeping a lock of a pet's hair, the most comforting was the pet keeper's belief that they would be reunited with their animal in the afterlife.[6]

Even people who aren't particularly religious are drawn to the promise of reunion because it's so comforting. John, one of the vet tech students I interviewed, said that although he's not religious, he still held tight to a vision of his dog Dare getting her "heart's desire in heaven." "I see her running through fields, hunting, doing what dogs love to do," he said. "It's a nice vision to have, so I more or less choose to see it that way, that she's at peace doing what she wants to do and waiting for the rest of us to show up."

The vision of an afterlife for animals that John described is more than a passing wish for many pet keepers. It is, in fact, a deeply felt need. As Gary Kurz writes in the popular book *Cold Noses at the Pearly Gates*, "Each of my departed pets left a permanent mark on my heart and a little more emptiness in my life. I love . . . each of them, and I do not want to forget them at any level. I don't appreciate someone suggesting that I should. Most pet lovers would agree that this is just not an option. We no more want to think 'that's it' for them than we want to believe 'that's it' for ourselves when we pass from this world."[7]

Research has shown that prayer or meditation has measurable health benefits. According to neuroscientist Andrew Newberg, "activity involving meditation and intensive prayer permanently strengthens neural functioning in specific parts of the brain that are involved with lowering anxiety and depression, enhancing social awareness and empathy, and improving cognitive and intellectual functioning."[8]

Unfortunately, as noted earlier, most religious institutions do not offer formal support for pet loss, and many people are reluctant to approach their religious leadership for help for fear of being judged. Yet I encourage you to do so. If you're active in a religious community, you might reach out to your religious leader and ask if they would mention your pet during prayers for the congregation or possibly offer a special chapel service on a monthly or bimonthly basis for pets who've been lost. There's always a chance your requests will be turned down, but you might also be pleasantly surprised by the support you receive. Pet loss has emerged as a serious issue in the last few decades, and religious leaders are becoming increasingly aware of the important role they can play in helping their congregants navigate the loss of *all* their family members, whether human or animal.

Keep a daily gratitude list
One of the best ways to boost your well-being while you're grieving is to regularly write down everything you feel thankful for in your life. This can include simple things, like the sound of birds in the morning or the taste of a fresh cup of coffee, but your list can also include big things, like having a loving spouse, a good job, or a friend who went out of their way to check in with you to see how you're doing. Writing down four or five things you're grateful for every day is sufficient.

You might also write down all the things you're grateful for about your pet. Even though they're no longer with you physically, your animal is still very present in your heart, and conscientiously acknowledging their gifts can gradually improve your physical and emotional well-being. You might feel at times that you're simply going through the motions because it can be difficult to truly feel grateful for a pet you've lost when you're overwhelmed with grief. Yet research has shown that behavior changes biology. As noted by one researcher, "writing a daily gratitude list for fourteen days was shown to have a positive effect on subjective happiness, life satisfaction, and a decrease of negative emotions or depressive symptoms."[9]

Engage in creative work
Many people benefit from expressive or artistic activities after losing a pet. This includes journaling, letter writing, poetry and memoir,

scrapbooking, drawing and painting, singing or composing a musical score, or other artistic work.

Journaling and letter writing can be especially healing. Writing is uniquely suited to articulating painful feelings that may seem fleeting or fuzzy, helping you untangle the confusing and overwhelming thoughts and emotions that characterize grief. Putting your thoughts and feelings down on paper can also be very liberating because it helps you get them out of your head so you can review them later. A journal or letters can be revisited as time goes by, helping you learn from your loss. When you review what you wrote immediately after your pet was lost and then again months later, you'll likely discover that your feelings have changed over time. This can alleviate any concerns you might have that you're "stuck" in your grief, a phrase we often hear when grief is long-lasting. When Kim McCool read her journal about her dog Holly more than ten years after Holly's death, she remarked that many emotions arose for her, both sweet and sorrowful. But above all, she was grateful she had this record, noting that "re-reading these pages reminded me of things I'd forgotten. I'm so glad I took the time to capture all of them!"

If you decide to try journaling, I encourage you to keep a notebook handy so you can jot down your thoughts as they come to mind. It also helps to write regularly at the same time every day, even if it's only for five or ten minutes, to clear your mind and calm your heart

Writing a letter to your pet can also be helpful, especially if you're struggling with guilt or remorse. You can write to your pet, or, alternatively, you can write a letter to yourself from your pet's perspective. This can help you get in touch with how deeply your pet loved you, and you might consider that your pet would want you to take good care of yourself as you navigate your grief journey.

Finally, drawing, painting, scrapbooking, and creating a photo album, either physical or digital, are wonderful ways to commemorate a pet, spark storytelling, and aid healing. These visual records will remind you of the many joyful or funny moments you shared with your animal. You can take on such projects at any time that feels comfortable to you. As I've said, you might find it too painful to look at pictures of your pet immediately after their death, but with time you're likely to discover that you can smile and laugh through your tears as you look at pictures of your pet and remember the good times you shared.

Share your story with others
Talking about your pet with people who understand what you're going through may be one of the most important things you can do when you're grieving. Elisabeth Kübler-Ross was a big advocate of storytelling as a coping strategy for loss. "Telling the story helps to dissipate the pain," she wrote. "Telling your story often and in detail is primal to the grieving process. You must get it out. Grief must be witnessed to be healed. Grief shared is grief abated. . . . Tell your tale, because it reinforces that your loss mattered."[10]

If your family and friends are supportive, I encourage you to talk about your pet for as long as they're willing to listen. It's not unusual, however, for people to grow impatient with your grief, unless they're grieving the loss of the same animal. Many people have told me their family and friends were supportive soon after their loss, but after three or four months, even the most supportive people became frustrated and impatient. If this happens to you, or if you struggle to find anyone who offers genuine and patient sympathy for your grief, I recommend attending a pet loss support group. Grief can make you feel crazy, and it can also make you feel very alone. Sharing your story with people who understand can help with both of these challenges.

Attending a group can be helpful no matter where you are on your grief journey. Soon after your loss, you might have a burning need to review the events and decisions that led up to your pet's death, and sharing your story with others can be cathartic. Attending a group is also helpful if you're struggling with the recurrence of "what if" and "if only" thoughts that consume your every waking moment. A group can also be helpful years after your loss as you begin to wrestle with the deeper meanings of your relationship with your pet. Some people have attended my pet loss support group off and on for years because they find it affirming and helpful, no matter where they are in their journey. Many find great satisfaction in supporting others and offering their own perspective as someone who has survived to tell the tale.

Perhaps the greatest benefit enjoyed by people who've attended my pet loss support group is the realization that they're not alone. A young man who regularly attended my group for more than a year offered this reflection on the experience:

> I'd never been in group therapy before, and I didn't think the group was going to be helpful. I was very surprised when it was. It did make me feel better because I realized I'm not the only one who feels this deeply and passionately about my animal. So the group felt like a safe place. Just being able to talk about the loss was helpful. Other people were talking too, and when I attended the group, there was this guy who had lost his dog a year ago and still came to the group. I was like, wow, his dog passed away a year ago, and he's still in a lot of pain. I think knowing that helped me give myself a little bit of forgiveness to let myself really feel what I felt.

• • •

In this chapter, we reviewed some of the challenges we face soon after the loss of an animal companion, such as deciding what to do with a pet's possessions, when to get another pet, and how to respond to the grief of other pets. We also reviewed some coping strategies you can use to process your emotions and manage your grief.

You might have noticed a remarkable similarity between the coping strategies discussed here and the continuing bond expressions presented in chapter 6. Saving keepsakes, conducting memorials, and building shrines are all expressions of the bond, and they're all important coping strategies as well. Whatever we might call them, these activities are not only beneficial but necessary to our grieving process. If we rush to rid our homes of a pet's possessions, change our routines, immediately get another pet, or otherwise attempt to quickly put the past behind us, we risk intensifying and prolonging our grief. But when we engage in activities that strengthen our bonds with our lost pets, we might enjoy many long-term benefits.

At the beginning of this chapter, you met Kim McCool, who kept a journal after the sudden loss of her dog Holly. By pouring her sorrow onto the page, Kim was able to experience her emotions while simultaneously giving them an outlet. And by recording all the small details of Holly's absence—the many reminders of the routines they'd enjoyed but could no longer enjoy—she began to appreciate the powerful role Holly played in her life and to explore the roots of her devotion to that little dog. In this way, the coping strategy Kim used to cope from one day to the next became a gateway to new learning and personal growth. As we conclude our journey through the long, winding valley of grief in the next two chapters, we'll take a closer look at what our losses can teach us about ourselves, about life and death, and about our animal friends.

CHAPTERS 6–7

Discussion Questions

1. Chapter 6 introduced the continuing bonds understanding of grief, which suggests that maintaining an emotional connection with a deceased loved one can be a healthy way to cope with loss. Tell a story about a pet, human loved one, or sacred place for whom you feel a continuing connection that describes the activities you engage in to maintain your connection.

2. Chapter 6 also discussed the experience of sensing a pet's continued presence, hearing a pet's sounds, catching brief glimpses of your pet, or having vivid dreams about a pet. Think about a time when you or someone you know experienced any of these. Describe the event, how you felt, and the meaning you made of it.

3. Chapter 7 explored the challenges we face soon after losing a pet, such as changes in our daily routines, deciding what to do with a pet's possessions, or whether (and when) to get another pet. Tell a story about the challenges you experienced following the loss of a pet or another loved one and the actions you took in response to these challenges.

4. Chapter 7 also discussed some coping strategies we use when we've lost a loved one, such as journaling, building a shrine, or conducting a memorial service. Think of a loss you've experienced and describe the strategies you used that helped and hindered your coping.

Transformation

CHAPTER 8

Making Meaning of Loss

When my coauthor Karen and I facilitated our online course in veterinary chaplaincy, we named our cohorts to honor animals on the endangered species list. In the spring of 2022, we had three small cohorts: the Kakapo Parrots, the Blue Whales, and the Hawksbill Sea Turtles. Each week, these groups would receive a new written lecture, much like the chapters in this book. They also responded to discussion questions in an online forum. Everyone read everyone else's stories and responded in a supportive way. The stories we shared and the warm, compassionate support we offered to each other forged tight bonds of shared experience and friendship.

Karen and I adored all the people we came to know in the five years we taught the course, but there was something special about the bond that formed among the people we met that spring. Some of our students eventually became our friends, including Linda Moore, who was a member of the Hawksbill Sea Turtles.

Linda was on her way to ordination as an Episcopal priest at the time, so she had a lot on her plate. She was working part time as a lab tech and serving as an apprentice priest. But she persisted through the course, even when her sister died unexpectedly. Shortly after graduation, Linda became an ordained priest and, within a year, launched the Abiding Ties Pet Loss Support Group. I was amazed by what Linda accomplished. I know from experience that launching a support group and getting the word out to your community is very challenging. But Linda was up for the challenge.

A warm, jovial woman, Linda was passionate about her faith and animals. When she was asked to share a story about a special pet, she wrote about Maggie, her yellow lab, the same dog who she believed sent her a message from the "other side" when she was cleaning out her car. Maggie had died after a long fight with cancer. The cancer took one of her legs but never her spirit. Here is an excerpt from Linda's dedication to Maggie's legacy:

> Maggie taught me how to stay in the now, to live in the present. When she developed osteosarcoma and her leg was amputated, I felt like I had mutilated my dog. But she bounced back to herself so much quicker than I would have if our places had been reversed. It was like she said, "Hey, this is no big deal. Watch my new hop-run." She still loved life. She still loved to roll in the mud, deer poop, and snow (sometimes all in the same day).
>
> Another special thing about Maggie was that sometimes she would have some trepidation about new things, and that won my heart because I have that too! When she was a puppy, I thought I would have to carry her up and down stairs all her life. Once she figured out stairs, though, she loved running up and down them. . . . She taught me to do new things. Even if you're scared, even if it takes multiple tries to do something, keep doing it. You'll probably learn you love it! This is a lesson I kept in mind throughout seminary and this veterinary chaplaincy course. Don't give up. Keep trying.
>
> Maggie also taught me to own my stubbornness and not apologize for it. She taught me to be courageous even when I'm scared to death. She taught me to never give up if you fail

on the first try. How often do I limit myself? How often do I not see the bigger picture? How often do I box myself in to "I can only do this; I can't do that?" These are the questions Maggie helped me to ask.

In chapter 6, I introduced the concept of continuing bonds, an understanding of grief that recognizes that we maintain emotional connections with our deceased loved ones and that such connections can be a healthy way to cope with loss. After a loss, we construct an internal, mental image of the deceased—essentially, a memory. This memory is dynamic, evolving over time. In the days, months, and years following our loss, we continue to interact with this memory, and our thoughts and feelings may gradually change as we revisit this memory with the knowledge and wisdom gained from new experiences. In the words of grief researchers Stephen R. Shuchter and Sidney Zisook, continuing bonds are "living and breathing" connections with the deceased.[1] They are not fixed entities but continue to change throughout our lives.

Linda's continuing bond with Maggie is a great example of this "living and breathing" connection. Her thoughts and feelings about her beloved dog changed over time. Initially, Linda was devastated by Maggie's death. Seven years later, she still felt wistful and sad when thinking about her struggle with cancer, but her heart was also full of love and gratitude for Maggie's life and the many gifts she'd received from Maggie. Today, Linda can laugh when she thinks about Maggie, and she enjoys telling stories about her fun-loving, quirky personality.

As Linda's story demonstrates, the journey of grief encompasses far more than coping with painful emotions and sensations until they fade. It's about finding meaning in loss and integrating those meanings into the complex story of our lives. Maggie became a part of Linda. Her loving nature, stubbornness, and courage are imprinted on Linda's heart. When Linda enrolled in my chaplaincy course and subsequently launched her pet loss support group, the love she continued to feel for

Maggie and the lessons she'd learned from that beautiful yellow lab sustained her.

The death of a loved one, including an animal, can be a pivotal moment in our lives. Losing those we love is painful and confusing, but these losses can also mark the beginning of a new chapter in our lives. Our losses transform us, often for the better, as we embrace new understandings of ourselves and the world. In this chapter, we'll take a close look at how this transformation occurs and the varied ways our pets change our lives.

What Is Meaning-Making?

In the context of grief and loss, *meaning-making* is the process by which people integrate the loss of a loved one into their lives and arrive at new understandings of those events and of themselves. This is a basic definition of the term, but to fully appreciate all that's involved in making meaning of our relationship with a lost loved one, I'd like to turn to the field of adult education.

Now, you might wonder what education has to do with grief, but it actually provides some very helpful insights. The field of adult education is concerned in part with how we acquire new learning. As we'll see in this discussion, the journey of grief is all about new learning.

According to education scholar Jack Mezirow, adults learn by reflecting on new experiences and ideas and weighing them against their current understanding of themselves and the world. "To make meaning means to make sense of an experience," writes Mezirow. "We make an interpretation of it. . . . What we perceive and fail to perceive and what we think and fail to think are powerfully influenced by habits of expectation that constitute our frame of reference, that is, a set of assumptions that structure the way we interpret our experiences. . . . Critical reflection involves a critique of the presuppositions on which our beliefs have been built."[2]

We all have habitual ways of thinking and acting. These habits of mind and behavior typically spring from the meanings and values we acquire in our families of origin and our culture. When new experiences support these meanings and values, our understanding of the world makes sense, and we feel good about who we are and what we believe. As we move through life, we generally dismiss troubling or irritating events and ideas that don't appear to fit our worldview. Most of the time, this is easy to do, like swatting away a buzzing insect. But when a new experience or idea is so upsetting that it directly challenges our beliefs, our thoughts and actions can become stuck. These are the moments when we experience what Mezirow calls a *disorienting dilemma*.[3] A disorienting dilemma is a disruptive experience that compels us to reflect critically on our common habits of mind.

I've experienced many disorienting dilemmas in my life, and I expect you have as well. Modern life is rife with conflict, contradiction, and constant change. In previous generations, someone might be born and die in the same community, maintaining close relationships with family and friends throughout their lives. Today, however, we're a highly mobile society. We move from city to city, region to region, or even country to country in search of adventure and opportunity or out of economic necessity. Our relationships tend to be transitory as well, and many of us can no longer rely on an extended family or a large group of friends to support us in our time of need.

On a macro scale, we also face disorienting dilemmas due to climate change, environmental destruction and contamination, the rapid extinction of millions of plant and animal species, rapid technological change, and political, economic, and social upheaval. All these issues and many others contribute to a malaise of uncertainty that afflicts almost everyone.

Another phrase for the habits of mind discussed here is *cognitive schema*. According to education scholar Julie Stern, a cognitive schema is a "mental structure [that] helps us understand how things work. It has to do with how we organize knowledge. As we take in new information, we connect it to other things we know, believe, or have experienced. And those connections form a sort of structure in the brain."[4] In other words, our worldview is hardwired into our brains.

Notably, brain imaging studies have shown that the loss of a loved one activates the same centers of the brain as new learning.[5] For more than two decades, psychologist Mary-Frances O'Connor has studied the effects of loss and grief on the human brain. She and her colleagues discovered that a loved one's absence causes a major disruption in the brain's neurological wiring. In an article about her work in *Scientific American*, O'Connor said her studies have found that our loved ones "are in the wiring of our brain. So when we fall in love with our baby or we fall in love with the person who becomes our spouse, it changes the wiring. It updates the physical connections between neurons, and it changes the way that proteins are folded."[6] In turn, when that loved one is lost, "Those physical traces in the brain have to be changed to reflect an updated understanding of the world, and that takes time. But it also takes experience. We have to have many, many days of being in the world without our spouse or our child or our best friend for the brain to create new connections and a new understanding of what it means to be without this person."[7]

Whether we're talking about the loss of a child, a spouse, a best friend, or a cherished pet, the neurological mechanism is the same. Because we're so accustomed to seeing our pets every day, adjusting to their absence can shock our neurological wiring. Creating new neural pathways entails adjusting to a new normal that no longer includes your animal. This is one of the reasons that grief can be so painful and can linger for such a long time. Indeed, grief is a physiological challenge as much as it is a spiritual and emotional one.

So how do we respond to disorienting dilemmas when they occur? Quite often, we simply refuse to change, instinctively clinging to our familiar beliefs and sometimes even distorting what happened to fit those beliefs. We also might carefully avoid any situation that induces the troubling sense that the world doesn't work the way we believe it should. As Mezirow notes, "When experience is too strange or threatening to the way we think or learn, we may block it out or resort to psychological defense mechanisms to provide a more compatible interpretation."[8]

But a disorienting dilemma can also compel us to question our assumptions about the world and ourselves. Sometimes, we respond by adjusting our foundational beliefs. Mezirow refers to this profound shift in our thinking and behavior as *transformative learning*.[9] This kind of learning involves far more than the accumulation of information; rather, it reflects a shift in our perception of the world, a rewiring of our neural pathways, and changes in our behavior. This is the complex process through which we grow and change throughout our lives, sometimes rejecting new ideas and beliefs and sometimes embracing them. As ironic as it might seem, we often learn and grow more from our disappointments and losses than from pleasurable experiences that reinforce our comfortable, habitual way of seeing the world.

When it comes to pet loss, a variety of scenarios can result in a disorienting dilemma, and sometimes we might be compelled to make major changes in our lives. As I've said, this transformative learning process can be painful, but it can also be incredibly rewarding.

How Losing a Pet Can Change Us

In chapter 3, I shared the story of Elaine and her dog Harvey. Harvey's accidental death by suffocation was traumatic for Elaine, and she said she felt broken inside. But she pushed through her pain, hour by hour, day by day, gradually rebuilding her life. She eventually emerged from the darkness that had completely enveloped her. In doing so, she gained a new understanding of her identity and a different perspective on life and death.

Elaine had lost many other loved ones in her life: her mother, sister, fiancé, other pets, and Harvey's brother, Stanley. All those loved ones had been sick prior to their passing, so their deaths had a rational explanation. Elaine grieved these losses, but she could accept them because they made sense. But Harvey's death was different.

"When Harvey's brother died, I was prepared because he had an injury, he had surgery, it progressed," Elaine said. "I had a chance to accept it. With Harvey, I had no chance. None. I went out, I came back, and it was all over. Same thing with my older female dog who passed away. This was after Harvey's death. She died in my arms. She had a stroke as I was rushing her to the vet. And even though I cried, it wasn't as devastating. I mean, she was old, and I saw how she was not living the best life. I could accept that because that's the natural course of things. But with Harvey, it was unnatural."

Harvey's sudden death challenged Elaine's long-held assumption about how the world should work. For Elaine, death was acceptable when it followed an illness, but it was unacceptable or "unnatural" when it arrived suddenly, without warning, and for no apparent reason. Confronting Harvey's sudden, senseless death forced Elaine to rethink her perspective on death and her priorities in life.

"Losing Harvey so suddenly has helped me be more in the moment," Elaine said. "I'm not so confident that tomorrow is going to be like today, so it makes me cherish today. What I have today—I can see it, I can touch it, I can feel it. But tomorrow, it may all be gone. So now I just stay in the day. I was never like that before. I was always someone who was thinking about the past or thinking about what I needed to do in the future, and I wasn't as in touch with this day. Now I am fully present every single day. I'm aware of every moment, and I make it a point to appreciate it."

When I reflect on my conversation with Elaine, I'm struck by how the stories she shared about Harvey had changed considerably from those she told when she first began attending my pet loss support group. At that point in her journey of grief and meaning-making, her perspective on her loss was framed almost solely by her pain. She talked a lot about the circumstances of Harvey's death: the series of actions that led to his death, the anger she felt toward her friend for bringing a plastic bag of treats into her home, and the guilt she felt for overlooking the fact that the bag was in Harvey's reach. She described her struggles at work and how hard it was to survive from one day to the next. When I spoke with her nine years later, her deep sorrow was still with her when she thought about Harvey's death, but she had also come to appreciate the special connection they shared, the lessons she learned from his death, and the grief that overwhelmed her life. Such insights were hard-won, but they helped Elaine find meaning in Harvey's death and the six wonderful years she enjoyed in his company.

How else might our interactions with our animal companions lead to disorienting dilemmas? One of the most common scenarios involves the lack of social support for pet loss. Say you confide in someone you trust about your intense feelings of sorrow for the loss of your pet. If that person minimizes your grief by suggesting, for example, that your grief is excessive or too long-lasting or that you should get another pet to feel better, you might question your beliefs about that person and your relationship with them. You might be inclined to withdraw from the relationship, believing they're not the supportive friend or family member you believed them to be. Conversely, you might doubt the validity of your own feelings, thinking that something must be psychologically wrong with you for grieving so intensely for an animal. You might even experience both emotions: alienation from your loved ones and self-doubt.

People who turn to their faith traditions for comfort and guidance might also experience a disorienting dilemma after losing a pet. As noted earlier, few religious institutions in the modern West provide formal support for pet loss, and people who love animals may feel alienated if their religious community seems indifferent to their suffering and, more broadly, to animal suffering in general. Christians might wonder why a God who is all-powerful and all-good would allow innocent animals to suffer as they do. They might also question the efficacy of prayer. Many wonder if they'll see their pet in the afterlife, yet Christianity offers inconsistent answers to this common concern. Some Christian leaders insist that animals don't ascend to heaven, while others may offer a tepid "maybe" because the Bible is unclear on the matter.

If a deeply religious person is told by their minister or priest that animals don't go to heaven, they might experience *religious disenfranchisement*, which I alluded to briefly in chapter 4. Like disenfranchised grief, religious disenfranchisement for pet loss is very real, though it's not widely acknowledged or well documented. I've met a few pet keepers who left their place of worship because of religious disenfranchisement, but I suspect that most people suffer in silence, keeping their feelings to themselves. Others go in search of answers, reading everything they can find about animals and the afterlife. Some of the most popular books about pet loss explore this topic, offering hope to people who draw comfort from the promise that they'll be reunited with their animal friends after they die.

The intensity of grief we suffer when we lose a pet can also be disorienting. Even the most devoted pet keeper may be surprised at how deeply they grieve for their animal. But why should we be surprised? Why is it that we expect to grieve less for our animals than for our human family members? I believe this phenomenon reflects the contradictory messages we receive about animals in our society. Yes, we consider our pets family members, but we've also been socially conditioned to believe that animals are lesser creatures than people and therefore less worthy of our love and sorrow. When confronted with a disorienting dilemma like this, you have a choice: question, adjust, or reject your feelings of love and attachment for your pet; or question, adjust, or reject popular beliefs about animals. I've met quite a few people whose beliefs about animals changed dramatically after they fell in love with a pet. Some even become involved in animal advocacy because of these experiences, while others have widened their circle of love to embrace all living creatures, even those we traditionally think of only as sources of food or labor.

No matter what form they take, the disorienting dilemmas we

experience when we lose a pet generally cause considerable discomfort and anxiety. Yet these experiences can also be positive and life affirming. Many pet keepers have told me that, although their grief journeys were incredibly difficult, they learned a great deal about themselves, animals, and the human-animal bond along the way. They became better people—wiser, more loving and patient with themselves and others, and more resilient.

Grief researchers have assigned a variety of names to this phenomenon, including *meaning reformation* and *posttraumatic growth*. The authors of a US study of pet loss noted that "the death of a beloved pet can be a turning point that alters one's perspective on life. Many people are able to transcend pain and turn crisis into opportunity while finding meaning out of the loss."[10] The authors also describe some of the positive changes we make in our lives following the death of a pet, including an "increased appreciation for life, more meaningful interpersonal relationships, an increased sense of personal strength, changed priorities, as well as a richer existential and spiritual life."[11] The study participants' responses are inspiring. "[Losing my pet] has tested the strength of my faith and reinforced my ability to maintain empathy and consideration for others despite my tremendous sense of loss and sadness," said one woman.[12] Another participant said that "each loss reminds me to value those in my life, to appreciate each one of them, humans and animals," while another said, "I have a fonder appreciation of all living creatures. I am less attached to material items and have a sense of connection to the universe."[13]

All the vet tech students I interviewed for my doctoral research study experienced what I would consider transformational learning because of their experiences with their special pets. The fact that they had dedicated their lives to healing animals and supporting their human guardians attests to the profound learning they experienced. Many shared important insights about animals, love, death, sorrow, and grief. Lillian described how she gained a new appreciation for person-pet relationships because of the profound connection she felt with her cat, Freddie. "My relationship with Freddie helped me understand more about the human-animal bond, from raising him as a kitten, all throughout his life, his death, and every step of the way throughout his whole life," Lillian said. "Because if you've never had that bond, you don't really understand when people refer to their dog as their baby or have cute, affectionate nicknames for their pets."

Frank shared a similar insight about the lessons he learned from his cat, Muppet. "The unconditional love I had with Muppet continues to educate me and show me how to be open to other animals, how to try to give more," Frank said. "We're human, and we make mistakes. We judge people. Even the best people judge people. But having unconditional love like that for a long time made me start trying to do it myself."

Frank also credits Muppet with teaching him important lessons about our responsibility to give the animals in our care a good quality of life. "When I was growing up [on the farm] and taking care of animals, I had to feed them and water them, but I didn't appreciate the quality of their life at the time," Frank said. "Well, there's a difference between giving basic care and giving quality of life. You can care for a human or an animal and give them the basic necessities. Or you can take that same person or animal and give them understanding and love and a good quality of life, and I think you get all of that back. Muppet taught me that."

Sometimes the insights we gain from our losses can arrive in an instant, especially during spiritual experiences, such as prescient dreams, inexplicable moments of synchronicity, and the comfort we draw from spiritual contemplation and immersion in the natural world. Most often, however, these insights emerge gradually as we work hard to make sense of new experiences. A pivotal life experience like the loss of a loved one can compel us to pause for a moment from the busyness of life and consider what is truly important to us. In the liminal space between what was and what will be, new learning and healing can unfold. As we carry on with our lives, we often recall the animals we've loved and lost while welcoming new ones into our lives. In this way, we spiral back and forth between past, present, and future in an intricate dance of meaning-making and transformative learning.

Sometimes the new learning and insights we gain after losing a pet change our lives for the better. When we're able to take the love we feel for our pets and pay that love forward to others, amazing things can happen. I call this forward-thinking response to loss *generativity*. I briefly introduced this concept in the discussion of continuing bonds in chapter 5. In the next chapter, I'll share the stories of people who've responded generatively to the loss of their animals and offer some final reflections on the long, winding valley of grief we've traveled in these pages.

CHAPTER 9

Generativity

Some would say that Lake Lure in Western North Carolina is heaven on earth. The lake is stunning, a mirror for the changing colors of the Carolina sky and the mountains and dense forests that surround its shores. In 2013, the town of Lake Lure converted an abandoned 155-foot span of US Memorial Highway 74 into a walking bridge, and local artists and gardeners created a unique garden that meanders across the bridge's three arches. Known as the "Flowering Bridge," it has attracted visitors from around the world.

In early 2022, Lake Lure became the home of another unique bridge. It measures about six feet wide and twenty feet long and is painted in festive shades of red, orange, yellow, blue, and green. This bridge is a real-world version of the magical gateway to pet heaven made famous by "The Rainbow Bridge" poem.[1] The poem offers a comforting vision of a land of rolling meadows where deceased pets romp and play, fully restored and free of pain, waiting for their human guardians to show up and continue their spiritual journey together.

Lake Lure's rainbow bridge is the creation of artist and woodworker Amy Wald, who wanted to create a lasting tribute to Barkley and Molly, two rescue dogs she lost during the COVID-19 pandemic. "During COVID, it was a tough time for everybody," Amy told me when I spoke with her. "I lost two pets and other people, and I was just sad. I read 'The Rainbow Bridge' poem, and I thought it was pretty. And I thought, why not make a real rainbow bridge? Because we all have little gravestones for our pets, or we have their ashes in an urn or something, or we have their collars. But just looking at those things on a shelf or their pictures on the wall didn't bring me any comfort. To me, it's just so sad, and I thought there's got to be a better way. I wanted to create something pretty where people can come when they've lost a pet. I wanted to do something to make it easier and better for others who've lost pets, a place I could share with other people who also feel that connection with their animals. When you come to the bridge and you see the funny, amazing things people say about their animals, you realize you have a community."

When the idea for the rainbow bridge first occurred to her, Amy said she thought for sure there must be rainbow bridges everywhere. "Every pet person knows about 'The Rainbow Bridge' poem," she said. "So I Googled it and was surprised because I couldn't find anything. I even had my grandkids search the internet for rainbow bridges because they're better at computer stuff than I am. But we couldn't find anything. And that's when I knew I just had to build one."

After obtaining permission from the town of Lake Lure for her project, Amy got to work. She didn't have any construction experience, but she'd done some woodworking and eventually found a kit that was easy and inexpensive to put together. After finishing the project, Amy hung Barkley's and Molly's collars on the bridge posts. A few of the volunteers who care for the plants on the Flowering Bridge added their pets' collars. Within a few weeks, word about Amy's rainbow bridge got around, and more people started going to Lake Lure to see the bridge and honor their pets.

A month or two after building the bridge, Amy did a few media interviews, and people soon began to show up in droves. Some traveled hundreds of miles to add a remembrance of their pet to the growing collection of collars, tags, laminated photos and messages, a hamster wheel and bird perch, and other keepsakes that festooned the bridge. Some collars held fifteen or twenty tags, a remembrance for every single dog and cat who brought joy to their human guardian.

Amy told me she loved watching people when they visited the bridge for the first time. Some cried, but it didn't take long for smiles and laughter to replace tears as they slowly wandered across the bridge, looking at the tags and photos and reading the tributes people had left for their animals. "Someone did a calculation for each pet that was on the bridge," Amy said. "Let's say each pet lives ten years. So that's 365 days, and they're probably in your lap or you're touching them or petting them for five hours a day. So that's ten times 365 times five. That's a lot of happy hours, a lot of love hours. We probably have a million love hours on that bridge."

Amy said she plans to build new rainbow bridges to fill what appears to be a deep need in the pet-keeping community. People need a "magical place," Amy said, to remember their animals, a place they can go and share their joys and sorrows with a community of people who love their animals as much as she does. "When you see all those collars and things on the bridge, you know you're not alone," Amy said. "When I visit the bridge, I think about all the pets I've loved and lost. It's not a sad place, not like a cemetery can be. It's a happy place. You can really feel it."

Amy's rainbow bridge is a wonderful example of a creative response to pet loss. When she built that bridge, Amy created something that helped people who grieve for their animal companions and have nowhere to take that grief. The fact that the bridge became a destination for pet keepers around the southeastern US and beyond attests to the need for a sacred place where people can honor their pets and share their memories with others.

Tragically, Lake Lure's rainbow bridge and the entire village of Chimney Rock, which is located just above Lake Lure on the Rocky Broad River, were destroyed by Hurricane Helene in the fall of 2024. I hold all the lives, both human and animal, that were lost in Western

North Carolina in my prayers. I know it will take many years for the region to recover from such devastation. Yet people are marvelously creative, and we often find surprising ways to bounce back from our losses. Indeed, only three weeks after the original rainbow bridge was destroyed, a new one was built at Lake Lure's town park, and plans are underway to completely rebuild both the flowering bridge and the rainbow bridge in their original locations.[2]

We can't control everything in our lives. We certainly can't control the forces of nature. Nor can we control death. But there are some things we can control. When it comes to losing a pet, the goal is to find something that appeals to you and suits your interests and talents. Amy's *something* was that beautiful rainbow bridge. She may even have sparked a trend. Maybe another pet keeper will follow her example and build a rainbow bridge in their community.

When Amy built that bridge, she engaged in what I call a generative response to death. Generativity is a forward-thinking response to death that honors the life of a loved one. It can manifest in many ways, though it is often expressed as a desire to help others and make the world a better place. In this way, our animals' loving spirits survive death. Our work in the world—or even our way of being in the world—can become their legacy.

Helping Yourself by Helping Others

One of the most tragic yet inspiring stories I've come across that demonstrates a generative response to the loss of an animal was shared by grief studies pioneer Elisabeth Kübler-Ross. In her last book, *On Grief and Grieving*, she shared stories about her childhood and the experiences that shaped her interest in helping grieving people.[3]

Elisabeth was the third of three girls born as triplets in 1926. She grew up in Zurich, Switzerland, and she and her sisters were something of a local sensation. Their images were featured on billboards around the city, and they were always dressed in matching outfits. It was challenging for young Elisabeth to develop a sense of her own identity, but her love of animals set her apart from her sisters. Elisabeth recalled that she had always loved animals, and as a child she enjoyed running a pretend animal hospital for all the critters she encountered outside, from birds to squirrels. She also shared the story of a rabbit named Blackie, whose tragic death changed her life:

> During my childhood we always had bunnies around the house, and I loved each and every one of them. The problem was my father was thrifty, and every six months he needed to roast a bunny for our dinner. I would have to bring the beloved bunnies, one by one, to the butcher. But I always made sure that my own special bunny, Blackie, was never chosen. He was mine, the one love object I had that belonged only to me.
>
> Blackie got fat because I kept giving him extra food, and of course the dreaded day came when my father told me it was time for me to bring Blackie to the butcher. I could not allow it. I begged Blackie to run away, but the more I shooed him away, the more he thought I was playing and would run back to me. No matter what I did he kept coming back, and my pain only escalated when I realized that he loved me too.
>
> The inevitable happened soon enough when my father sent me off with Blackie, making me promise to give him to the butcher. I did it, crying the whole time, and in a few minutes, out came the butcher with my dead Blackie in a bag.
>
> "Here's your rabbit," he said, handing it over. I felt catatonic when I reached out to accept it. I could still feel Blackie's warmth when the butcher remarked, "By the way, it's a damn shame you brought this bunny in now. It was a girl and in a day or two it would have had babies." That night at dinner, when my family ate Blackie, in my eyes they were cannibals.

But I would not cry for this bunny or anyone else for almost forty years.[4]

In concluding her story, Kübler-Ross explained that it took many years and a lifetime of work for her to make the connection between her love of Blackie, the rabbit's horrific death, and her lifelong dedication to helping people navigate their grief. "The repression of my grief for that bunny was instrumental in my reaching out to others to find their own," she wrote. "In this way I indirectly healed my own grief little by little."

Kübler-Ross struggled mightily with her grief for Blackie. She didn't speak about this experience for more than seventy years. Yet her dedicated service to helping people struggling with death and grief speaks loudly. It speaks to the beautiful truth that helping others is one of the best ways to help yourself. I sometimes wonder whether this amazing woman would have accomplished so much in her life if not for Blackie.

Though horrific, Kübler-Ross's story about Blackie is also instructive. It demonstrates the profound impact animals can have on our lives. It's also a testament to the resilience of the human heart. For me, the most inspiring takeaway is how Kübler-Ross transformed her grief for Blackie into a lifelong dedication to helping others. Her love of her pet bunny and her unresolved grief for Blackie's cruel death stayed with her throughout her life and set the direction for a career focused on helping people navigate death and grief.

Like many who enter helping professions, Kübler-Ross was a wounded healer. As a child, she was powerless to save her beloved Blackie. But as an adult, she was able to channel the sorrow and anger she suffered when Blackie died into her life's work. When we lose significant others, our love for them stays with us, and when we find ways to express that love in the world, it can be incredibly healing for ourselves and others.

Always in Your Heart—and in the World

We may be powerless over death, but we do have power over how we respond to death, and the loss of an important loved one can strengthen and focus this sense of empowerment. When we reach the point in our grief journey where our sorrow, guilt, and anger begin to ease, we might discover that the joy and love we shared with our pets are still very much alive. Those wonderful connections are still with us and always will be. If we're eventually able to take these gifts and share them with others—fanning them out like the fertile soil in a river delta—then we will have responded to death and suffering in a generative way.

I'm continually amazed by how love and meaningful connections with others can empower us to thrive, even after the most tragic losses. The love we feel for our pets is more powerful than death itself, and in the long run, it's this love that sustains and strengthens us. Love is the engine of generativity, and I believe that anyone who has enjoyed the nonjudgmental love of an animal companion has the potential to respond to the loss of that animal in a generative way.

Sometimes, we engage in generative acts as a way of atoning for our perceived responsibility for a pet's death. Celeste, one of the vet tech students I interviewed, attributed her work in veterinary medicine and her participation in animal rescue to her desire to atone for the guilt she felt for the suffering and death of her dog Rambo and other animals in her care. "I wanted to go into animal rescue because of what I saw Rambo and other animals go through," Celeste said. "I think I was put on the Earth like St. Francis or Noah or somebody like that where I think my whole job on Earth is to help the animals. And that's it. That's all I'm here for."

A graduate of my veterinary chaplaincy course, Bob Coulson, attributed his interest in this new field of spiritual care to his dog Pixie. After completing the course, Bob organized an animal kinship ministry at his church and developed a course on animal theology. "I do this in honor of Pixie's memory," Bob said. "Pixie taught me about love and grief—what I would call the real mind-numbing, heartbreaking, spirit-crushing grief that makes you feel like you're losing your mind. I wanted to honor her spirit and what she taught me, and I'm trying to do that by helping people love their pets better and more fully and understand what that love bond is all about."

The beautiful thing about generativity is that it can be expressed in many ways. You don't have to change the world to keep your pet's loving spirit alive. Even small gestures can have a big impact on the people and animals you share your life with, and you never know how your compassionate actions will ripple out and influence others. You might resolve to be a kinder, more compassionate person or to follow the example of your animal friends and live in the world with more generosity and less judgment. Perhaps you post an online memorial for your pet or write words of sympathy in response to someone else's post. Holding a memorial or ritual ceremony for a pet is a wonderful way to say to the world, "This animal mattered!" You might also find it helpful to join a pet loss support group, both to address your own grief and offer your support to others.

The creative ways we find to respond to our losses are deeply personal, and you must find what speaks to your heart. When we respond in a generative way, we heal our hearts and renew our spirits through a deep and satisfying sense of meaning and purpose. Our animals live on *in* us and *through* us in how we lead our lives, in our volunteer activities, and in our work.

Navigating the long, winding valley of grief is perhaps best understood as learning how to suffer. Our losses inevitably bring suffering. But through suffering, we can grow, learn, and transform ourselves and, within the limits of our resources and ability, also transform the world around us. When framed in this way, a loved one's death can be appreciated as an opportunity for lasting spiritual growth and personal transformation. Our joyful memories of our pets and the love we continue to feel for them can transform our lives and compel us to seek ways to pay the love forward. It can take many years to fully appreciate the everlasting bounty of the human-animal bond. My hope is that you're able to cherish your memories of all your lost loved ones with joy and gratitude.

The spiritual journey we undertake after losing the people, animals, and things we love never really ends. Our path becomes their legacy. In a very real sense, we speak on our pets' behalf in the way we live our lives—in the love, tolerance, and humility we bring to our relationships, in the intention to bring joy and gratitude to each moment of our day, and in our grace and courage in the face of death. We can strive to take the best of what we've received from our pets and carry it forward. In this way, we honor the lives and spirits of our animal friends. If we live into this goal with great intention, we can discover that our dogs, cats, horses, birds, snakes, lizards, hamsters, fish, and all the other wonderful creatures who we're lucky enough to know well are truly remarkable. We're lucky to have them as our teachers about what's truly important.

CHAPTERS 8–9

Discussion Questions

1. Chapter 8 explored meaning-making and introduced the concept of a disorienting dilemma, which is an event that challenges your worldview. Tell a story about a time when you experienced a disorienting dilemma that led to a major shift in your perspective about yourself, other people, animals, or your understanding of how the world works.

2. Chapter 9 reviewed the concept of generativity, which is a creative, life-affirming response to loss that seeks to honor a loved one's memory. Tell a story about how you or someone you know responded to a loss in a generative way.

3. Chapter 9 acknowledged the difficulty of death and loss but also the value of expressing gratitude for the gifts our loved ones have brought to our lives. Reflect on a pet, a human loved one, or a sacred place, and describe what you're grateful for.

The Sacred Story Project

CHAPTER 10

Crafting Your Sacred Story: Connecting and Coping

The concept of the sacred story was introduced in *Heart Animals*, the first book in the Pet Chaplain Learning Series. A sacred story is a personal narrative that speaks to your deeply held values and beliefs and your sense of meaning and purpose. The goal of crafting a sacred story about your relationship with animals is to explore some fundamental questions: What are your core values and beliefs about animals and the natural world? How have your experiences with animals and the people in your life shaped these values and beliefs? What sparked your interest in the learning series, and what are your hopes for your future in relationship with animals and your fellow human beings?

The sacred story project is a progressive writing exercise, and installments appear in each book in the series. The exercise presented here is the second round of the sacred story project and invites you to focus on your social experiences around the loss of a special pet. If you've completed the first two rounds of the sacred story project, you can integrate the story or stories you've already composed with the story you write here. Alternatively, you might choose to write about a different topic.

The sacred story project is a progressive writing exercise, and installments appear in each book in the series. The exercises presented here represent the second round of the sacred story project and invite you to focus on your connection with your loved one and the creative ways you've found to cope with their loss. As discussed in *Heart Animals*, these topics correspond to the first and second domains of the 3 Chaplain Cs Method of Storytelling, or the 3 Chaplain Cs for short. The 3 Chaplain Cs is an interview framework I developed for supporting grieving pet keepers, and it includes three domains:

- Connecting with a loved one
- Coping creatively with the loss of that loved one
- Communication with others about the loved one

The organizational framework of the learning series is based on these three domains. The first chapter in this book, "Our Animal Teachers," addresses the first domain, and the remaining chapters explore the second domain. You can write a separate story for each of these domains or a single story that encompasses both. You can also choose to write separate stories about different topics. For example, you might write a story about your connection with one pet and a different story about how you coped with the loss of a different pet.

If you plan to read the other books in the series, I recommend holding onto the story or stories you compose now for later use. The third domain of the 3 Chaplain Cs—communicating with others—is the focus of the third book in the series, *Just an Animal*, and you'll have the opportunity to write about your social experiences relative to your pet. You might want to incorporate whatever you create now with the story or stories you create after finishing the third book. For those of you who plan to read *Veterinary Chaplaincy*, the fourth book in the series, you'll have the opportunity to pull everything you've written for the sacred story project in the first three books into a clear statement of your calling to this new field of spiritual care.

If you haven't completed the first and second rounds of the sacred story project, you can still complete this exercise. You might wish to expand your story beyond your social experiences to include other aspects of the relationship you've chosen to write about, such as your sense of connection to a pet, the circumstances of their loss, the strategies you used to cope with your grief, and the lessons you learned from that experience. Because the learning series is focused on pet keeping and loss, I encourage you to write a pet who was particularly important to you. But you can write about any relationship or experience you feel is relevant to your spiritual development and identity. The goal of the learning series is, in part, to help you appreciate your connection with the greater-than-human world. Many people who love animals and grieve their loss also grieve the rapid loss of flora and fauna in the modern age. If you feel moved to write about a champion tree and the grief you felt when it was cut down, then please do so. You also might write about the people in your life, particularly if they influenced your relationship with animals.

Whatever approach you take, be sure to include any spiritual experiences related to the relationship or experience you've chosen to write about. Therapist Pamela A. Hays describes significant spiritual events as "shimmering moments," and this simple phrase captures the unique quality of the experiences that demand our attention and evoke feelings of awe and wonder.[1] Your reflections might include spiritual experiences concerning your pet during their lifetime and following their loss, such as dreams that were particularly memorable or prescient; moments of inexplicable synchronicity; times when you felt a particularly strong sense of awe through a sacred connection with your pet; an occasion when you sensed your deceased pet's physical presence; and prayers, rituals, and other activities you engaged in following their loss that you consider to be sacred.

Revisiting your memories of a lost loved one is not an easy task, so it's important to practice good self-care during this process. Be gentle with yourself as you work on your sacred story. Cry or rage when you need to, and allow yourself to feel your feelings. Keep a journal and note whatever arises for you. Practice good self-care by getting plenty of rest, eating healthfully, and exercising. If you feel upset or anxious, take a walk, listen to your favorite music, engage in a relaxing hobby, write in your journal, pray, or meditate—whatever works for you. Above all, I encourage you to reach out to supportive family, friends, or a professional caregiver if you need to share your thoughts and feelings during this process.

Finally, I'd like to emphasize that, although this exercise is grounded in writing practice, feel free to make it your own. You might wish to engage in other creative activities that complement your written work. If you're crafty, for example, you could create a scrapbook of photos and other memorabilia related to your chosen topic. Videos, slide shows, and music are great mediums for capturing our experiences. You also might select or compose poems and prayers or create a ritual that honors your animal. Do what feels right for you.

Writing Prompts

The following prompts might give you some inspiration for your story about your social experiences. These prompts concern a pet but can be adapted to whatever it is you've chosen to write about. I also recommend reviewing your answers to the discussion questions presented throughout this book.

Connecting with your loved one: the first domain

The following prompts can give you some inspiration for your story of connection. These prompts concern a pet but can be adapted to whatever it is you've chosen to write about.

- What did your pet look like? Briefly describe your pet's physical characteristics.
- How would you describe your pet's personality? What was special or unique about them?
- How did your pet come into your life and how long were they with you?
- What were some of your favorite activities with your pet?
- What did you value most about your pet?
- How did your life change because of your animal?
- What did you learn about who you are as an individual and what you value and believe in from your relationship with your pet?

While your story of connection might focus on positive experiences with your pet, I suggest including challenging experiences as well. The truth is that our relationships with our animal companions are not always happy. Keeping pets can be messy, expensive, and physically and emotionally challenging, and some pets have behavioral issues that can be difficult to deal with. Moreover, you might find that some of your interactions with your pet evoke both positive and negative feelings. For example, you might love your dog's playfulness and curiosity, but you might also have felt frustrated when that playfulness and curiosity resulted in a mound of shredded toilet paper in your bathroom. You might also feel guilty because of an interaction with your pet that you came to regret later, and writing about these experiences can help you process your feelings.

Coping creatively with the loss of your loved one: the second domain

The following prompts may give you some inspiration for a story about coping with the loss of your pet. Be sure to incorporate any lessons or significant meanings that emerged from your grief journey.

- When did you last see your pet? Describe what they looked like and the thoughts and feelings that arise for you when you think about that moment.

- What were the circumstances of your loss? You might find it helpful to write at length about the events that led to the loss of your pet, especially if your loss was recent. The death of a loved one—or the loss of a sacred place—can be a momentous, life-changing experience, and a careful review of the details surrounding your loss can help you process your grief.

- What activities did you engage in after losing your loved one? What helped and what hindered your ability to cope with your volatile emotions?

- How has your life changed because of your loss and grief journey thus far?

- What insights did you gain because of this experience into who you are as an individual and what you value and believe?

- Describe a few generative ways you might "pay the love forward" and honor your animal's legacy?

Writing Guidelines, Tips, and Suggestions

If you have trouble getting started or feel stuck at any point in your writing process, the following guidelines, tips, and exercises may be helpful. These also appear in *Heart Animals*, so if you've already read that book, you can skip this material.

Define your guiding purpose

Establishing an overall goal for your narrative may give you some direction. For example, if you'd like to explore your experiences as a pet keeper and animal lover, you might write about one or two special pets. If you're an animal caregiver who works in the veterinary field or animal rescue, you might focus on the relationships and experiences that compelled you to enter your field. If you're interested in the practice of veterinary chaplaincy, you might consider all the significant relationships and experiences that have brought you to this book. You can then pull all this work together to create a clear, focused statement about your interest in interfaith spiritual care for pet loss.

Do some brainstorming

If you have trouble deciding what to write about, I suggest making a list of all the relationships and events that you believe have shaped your love of animals and, if you'd like, your interest in the practice of veterinary chaplaincy. Your list might include interactions with special pets, the important people in your life, memorable experiences in nature, significant milestones in your spiritual life, and so on. The entries on your list do not need to be lengthy descriptions but should include as much detail as you need to make sense of them later. This list provides an at-a-glance summary of the significant relationships and events you might want to write about.

Next, select a single entry from this list that rises above all the others in significance and make three additional lists about that relationship or event. These lists should include your reflections on the significance of that relationship, how you coped with the loss of your loved one, and your social experiences surrounding their loss. The goal is to jot down every shimmering moment you can recall about your chosen topic and the thoughts and feelings associated with those memories. You can add to these lists at any time and use them as a reference when composing your story or stories.

Alternatively, you could create a chronological timeline that includes the same information described here. A timeline can help you reconstruct your memory of key events in your life and see them in relation to one another. It's a great way to get a snapshot of the significant milestones of your spiritual journey thus far.

Some thoughts on revisiting your past

A common bit of wisdom shared by people working on their memoirs is to write from the scar, not the open wound. Time tends to buffer our strong emotions, and we can generally gain a fresh perspective on our losses when our most intense grief has eased. By examining your losses and other life-changing events after some time has passed, you'll be better able to articulate the lessons they hold for you. You'll also be better able to attend to others with the knowledge you've gained from self-reflection, which is particularly important if you're interested in chaplaincy. In the words of Buddhist author Lodro Rinzler, "Once [our] wound has scarred over, we are in fact the best people to talk to others about how to heal from similar situations, because we have been there and learned from it. We know the pain of that wound well and can hold space for other people to be present to it, without judgment."[2]

If you decide to write about a pet, your instinct might be to choose one you've recently lost, especially if that pet was very important to you. However, it might be best to select a pet who was lost at least three months ago. When I interviewed the vet tech students for my doctoral research, they were required to discuss pets they'd lost at least one year before their interview. The powerful meanings they shared with me likely took many months, if not years, to emerge. Many people who've lost pets in childhood or young adulthood were never given the opportunity to unpack those losses, and a great deal of personal insight and growth can be gained by revisiting them. If you want help reconstructing your memories, consider talking with family members or others who knew you and your pet.

Get visual

Visual aids can be helpful throughout the writing process. If you've chosen to write about a pet, looking at pictures or videos of your animal can help jog your memory. As noted earlier, if your pet was recently lost, you might find that you're overwhelmed with grief when you look at pictures or revisit your memories. This is natural and normal. Even joyful moments can be difficult to revisit when your loss is fresh and your grief intense. Again, be sure to practice good self-care during this process.

Write from your heart
In the book *Writing Down Your Soul*, author Janet Conner asserts that writing is one of the best ways to make meaning of our experiences and connect with what she calls the "Divine Voice" of wisdom and understanding that resides in all of us.[3] "There is a Voice inside you," Connor writes. "There is a Voice inside everyone. Whether you hear it or not, the Voice is there. Whether you ask for help or ignore its guidance, the Voice is still there. Waiting. It is waiting for you to stop, if just for a moment, and listen. The Voice is always there, guiding you, encouraging you, loving you."[4]

The sacred story project can help you connect with your voice or, as Conner phrases it, "penetrate the thin wall of consciousness that keeps you apart" from your inner voice.[5] Other activities can help you connect with your voice, including prayer, meditation, time spent in nature, and creative work such as the visual arts, music, and dance. But research has shown that there's something unique about the way our brains are wired that makes writing especially effective for new learning and meaning-making.[6]

If writing is difficult for you or you worry that you're not a good writer, your story might flow better when you describe your experiences out loud. Many recording and transcription tools are available to help you quickly convert your spoken story into written form. Remember, too, that your sacred story doesn't have to be perfect. Relax, let your words flow, avoid editing your story as you go, and see what arises. You might be surprised at what emerges if you release the "Divine Voice" within.

Immerse yourself in a single moment in time
A good way to jump-start your writing process and tap into your

divine inner voice is to focus on a single memory that is particularly meaningful to you. You can then expand your story from there. If you're writing about a pet, this might be the occasion when someone was particularly sympathetic and helpful after you lost your pet. Alternatively, you could focus on an interaction with someone that was especially stressful or difficult.

The following immersive writing exercise is designed to focus your attention on a specific time and place and put yourself in the scene. I used this method when composing my sacred story about my dog, Queenie, which appears in *Heart Animals*. It proved to be a powerful way to engage with my past, especially because Queenie died when I was very young.

In brief, you'll write continuously for a set length of time without stopping. I suggest starting with a half hour to see how it feels, but you can shorten this time to fifteen or twenty minutes if you wish. As you write, it's essential to turn off your inner critic. Don't worry about grammar, punctuation, or the organization of your story. If you're writing by hand, don't lift your pen or pencil from the page. Let your mind relax, and your thoughts and feelings flow. Write down whatever comes into your mind, even if it seems repetitive or off topic.

To begin the exercise, find a comfortable place to work, free from distractions and interruptions. I suggest muting your cell phone or leaving it in another room. Set a timer, take some deep breaths, relax your body, close your eyes for a moment, and bring your selected memory to mind. Begin by writing about the physical sensations that you experienced in that moment. Where are you? What things do you see around you? What time of day is it? What season is it? What do you see, hear, taste, smell, and feel on your skin? Is it hot, warm, cool, or cold where you are? Is the wind blowing? Are there others there with you? What happened? Be sure to describe the emotions you experienced as your story unfolds. Were you happy, sad, angry, elated, lonely, or some other feeling, or did you experience a mixture of emotions?

When the time is up, take a break, then review what you've written and make any edits you feel are necessary for clarity and narrative flow.

Wrapping it up

After completing a draft of your story, you might decide that you're happy with your story and feel no need to change it. I've found, however, that the editing process can be a learning experience in and of itself. As you review what you've written, other memories, thoughts, and feelings may arise, offering new insights into the meaning of your past relationships and experiences. It can even be helpful to set your story aside for a while and return to it later. The stories we tell about our past lives are always evolving as we experience new things and engage in new relationships. Those narratives are always with us, informing us and guiding us in life. They're forever a part of who we are, and I hope this exercise has helped you see your past experiences and yourself in a new way.

Our Journey Continues

In this book we've explored the long, winding valley of grief we travel when we lose a cherished pet. Navigating the loss of a pet can be a struggle, in part because it's so misunderstood and the support networks we rely on when we lose a human loved one are absent or hard to find. I cannot overstate the profound influence of our social world on the pet loss experience. To give this topic the attention it deserves, the next book in the Pet Chaplain Learning Series, *Just an Animal: Reflections on the Human-Animal Bond and Western Culture*, is dedicated to exploring how our social interactions and our culture shape the experience of loving and losing an animal companion. I invite you to continue your spiritual journey with me for a critical look at our cultural history and the profound ways our religious traditions, philosophical ideas, and scientific perspectives have shaped the way we think about and interact with the animals in our midst.

Acknowledgments

Many acquaintances, friends, and colleagues have contributed to the creation of the Pet Chaplain Learning Series. First, we'd like to recognize the team of advisors who generously dedicated their time and expertise to this project. Your enthusiasm for our work and unfailing encouragement buoyed our spirits when we felt overwhelmed by the vast scope of this project. A big thanks to Rev. Jayne Helgevold, hospice chaplain and pet foster mom; Eileen Medeiros, a college English professor and pug enthusiast; Rev. Linda Moore, Episcopal priest, chaplain, and lifelong animal lover; Nancy Osborne, retired hospital chaplain and Clinical Pastoral Education (CPE) supervisor; Fran Prem, who plans and coordinates CPE programs in Australia; and veterinarian Christine Scott. We're especially grateful to Fran for her detailed edits and astute feedback and the extra time and care she put into this project.

We'd also like to applaud the contributions of Kim McCool, who founded a pet ministry at St. John Vianney Catholic Church in Bettendorf, Iowa, shortly after completing our course. Kim is doing amazing things in her community and is truly an inspiration to us.

The learning series would not be what it is today without the input of all the students who participated in our veterinary chaplaincy course. Thank you to those who agreed to let us include your stories and reflections, and we'd like to give an extra big shout-out to Bob Coulson, Mary DeRosa, and Cindi Rodriguez as well as North Carolina artist Amy Wald for interviewing with us. By graciously allowing us to share your stories with our readers, you've had a positive ripple effect on all the people who will recognize themselves in your tales. And, of course, the learning series might not exist at all without the vet tech students who shared their stories with us. Their moving tales about your heart animals were the spark that compelled us to create the series.

In addition, we'd like to recognize the contributions of two scholars who are experts in the work of cultural anthropologist Ernest Becker, whose ideas about death anxiety are discussed in the third and fourth books in the series: Daniel J. Liechty, emeritus professor of social work at Indiana State University in Terre Haute, Indiana; and Sheldon Solomon, professor of psychology at Skidmore College in Saratoga Springs, New York.

A big thanks to our family and friends who cheered us on over the years; your interest and encouragement mean the world to us. We're especially indebted to our friend Larry Robinson. Larry, far too often, we ended up bending your ear as we mulled over the many decisions we needed to make in creating an online course followed by a book series. Your stalwart support and friendship—and the many fine dinners we enjoyed in your company—helped sustain us through this challenging journey.

Finally, and most important of all, we'd like to thank the many animals who've touched our lives and helped us become better people.

About the Authors

Rob Gierka holds a bachelor's degree in rhetoric and communications from Albany State University, a master's degree in technical writing from Rensselaer Polytechnic Institute, and a doctoral degree in professional and continuing adult education from North Carolina State University with a research focus on the human-animal bond and pet loss. Professionally, Rob enjoyed an eclectic career in communications, serving in various positions in private and public institutions before retiring in June 2016. He got his start in chaplaincy in the early 1990s when he took an extended unit of Clinical Pastoral Education at Rex Hospital in Raleigh, North Carolina, where he subsequently served as a volunteer chaplain for two years. While in training, Rob also served for a year as a Stephen Minister and for three years as chair of the congregational care committee at Pullen Baptist Church in Raleigh. In 2004, he launched the Pet Chaplain organization and began providing interfaith spiritual support to pet keepers in his community. Between 2004 and 2006, he served as the on-call chaplain at the Veterinary Teaching Hospital at North Carolina State University, and in 2006 he launched a pet loss support group at the Raleigh location of the Society for the Prevention of Cruelty to Animals.

Rob's life partner and coauthor Karen Duke holds a bachelor's degree in English from the University of Florida. She enjoyed a successful career as a writer and graphic designer before retiring in October 2021 and devoting her talents to the development of the learning series.

Notes

Introduction

1. C. S. Lewis, *A Grief Observed* (Bantam Books: 1976 [1961]), 69.
2. Lisa Irish, *Grieving—The Sacred Art: Hope in the Land of Loss* (Turner Publishing Company, 2018), xi-xii, Kindle.

Chapter 1: Our Animal Teachers

1. Robin Wall Kimmerer, *Braiding Sweetgrass: Indigenous Wisdom, Scientific Knowledge, and the Teachings of Plants* (Milkweed Editions, 2013), 9.
2. Elizabeth Barrett Browning, *Sonnets from the Portuguese and Other Poems* (Dover Publications, 1992 [1906]), 41–42.
3. Froma Walsh, "Human-Animal Bonds II: The Role of Pets in Family Systems and Family Therapy," *Family Process* 48, no. 4 (2009): 482, http://dx.doi.org/10.1111/j.1545-5300.2009.01297.x.
4. James Serpell, "Anthropomorphism and Anthropomorphic Selection–Beyond the 'Cute Response,'" *Society & Animals* 11, no. 1 (2003), 83–100, http://dx.doi.org/10.1163/156853002320936926.
5. Sandra B. Barker and Randolph T. Barker, "The Human–Canine Bond: Closer Than Family Ties?," *Journal of Mental Health Counseling* 10, no. 1 (1988): 46–56.
6. Anita M. Covert et al., "Pets, Early Adolescents, and Families" in *Pets and the Family*, ed. Marvin B. Sussman (Routledge, 1985): 95–108, https://doi.org/10.4324/9781315784656.
7. Marc Bekoff, *The Emotional Lives of Animals: A Leading Scientist Explores Animal Joy, Sorrow, and Empathy—and Why They Matter* (New World Library, 2010).
8. Marc Bekoff, *The Emotional Lives of Animals*, 27.
9. Jon Katz, *Soul of a Dog: Reflections on the Spirits of the Animals of Bedlam Farm* (Random House, 2009), 139, Kindle.
10. Jon Katz, *Soul of a Dog*, 139, Kindle.
11. Iris Smolkovic, Mateja Fajfar, and Vesna Mlinaric, "Attachment to Pets and Interpersonal Relationships," *Journal of European Psychology Students* 3, no. 1 (2012): 15–23, https://doi.org/10.5334/jeps.ao.
12. Caroline Knapp, *Pack of Two: The Intricate Bond Between People and Dogs* (Random House, 2010), 8.

13. Annett Schirmer, Ilona Croy, and Rochelle Ackerley, "What Are C-tactile Afferents and How Do They Relate to 'Affective Touch'?," *Neuroscience & Biobehavioral Reviews* 151 (2023), https://doi.org/10.1016/j.neubiorev.2023.105236.

14. Daisy Yuhas, "The Psychology of Pets," *Scientific American MIND*, May/June 2015, 32.

15. British psychologist and psychoanalyst John Bowlby is recognized as the first attachment theorist. His 1969 groundbreaking work *Attachment and Loss* (London: Basic Books) has been highly influential in the study of attachment between people and their pets.

16. Marilyn J. Kwong and Kim Bartholomew, "'Not Just a Dog': An Attachment Perspective on Relationships with Assistance Dogs," *Attachment & Human Development* 13, no. 5 (2011): 422, https://doi.org/10.1080/14616734.2011.584410.

17. Kai Epstude and Johanna Peetz, "Mental Time Travel: A Conceptual Overview of Social Psychological Perspectives on a Fundamental Human Capacity," *European Journal of Social Psychology* 42, no. 3 (2012): 269–275, https://doi.org/10.1002/ejsp.1867.

18. American Pet Products Association, "Current Trends in U.S. Pet Ownership," PDF downloaded January 2023. To view the latest research from the APPA, go to https://americanpetproducts.org/research-insights.

19. Gail Melson, *Why the Wild Things Are: Animals in the Lives of Children* (Harvard University Press, 2009), 34.

20. Froma Walsh, "Human-Animal Bonds II: The Role of Pets in Family Systems and Family Therapy," *Family Process* 48, no. 4 (2009): 481–499, http://dx.doi.org/10.1111/j.1545-5300.2009.01297.x.

21. Michael Schaffer, *One Nation Under Dog: Adventures in the New World of Prozac-Popping Puppies, Dog-Park Politics, and Organic Pet Food* (Holt, 2009), 18, Kindle.

22. Melinda Houston, "Fur Babies: Why Treating Our Dogs Like Our Kids Is Bad for Everyone," *The Sydney Morning Herald*, April 21, 2017, https://www.smh.com.au/national/fur-babies-why-treating-our-dogs-like-our-kids-is-bad-for-everyone-20170413-gvkgxx.html.

23. Stanley Coren, "In the Human Brain, Dogs and Children Are Equally Lovable," *Psychology Today*, January 7, 2015, https://www.psychologytoday.com/us/blog/canine-corner/201501/in-the-human-brain-dogs-and-children-are-equally-lovable.

24. Stanley Coren, "In the Human Brain, Dogs and Children Are Equally Lovable."

25. American Pet Products Association, "Current Trends in U.S. Pet Ownership," PDF downloaded January 2023. To view the latest research from the APPA, go to https://americanpetproducts.org/research-insights.

26. Froma Walsh, "Human-Animal Bonds II: The Role of Pets in Family Systems and Family Therapy," *Family Process* 48, no. 4 (2009): 481–499, http://dx.doi.org/10.1111/j.1545-5300.2009.01297.x.

27. Best Friends Animal Society, "October 2023 Blessing from Angels Rest," Video, 18:42, https://www.youtube.com/watch?v=EOeKFHrDoAo&list=PL7hRNs_gx88_ovjrHVpfUoAdP5ZuYXcgr&index=13.

Chapter 2: The Hardest Goodbye

1. Erich Lindemann, "The Symptomatology and Management of Acute Grief," *American Journal of Psychiatry* 101, no. 2 (1944): 141–148, https://doi.org/10.1176/ajp.101.2.141.

2. R. Scott Nolen, "Caring Too Much? At Teaching Hospital, Committee Tackles Ethical Issues of Veterinary Treatment," American Veterinary Medical Association, April 25, 2018, https://www.avma.org/javma-news/2018-05-15/caring-too-much.

3. Caroline Hewson, "Grief for Pets—Part 1: Overview and Some False Assumptions," *Veterinary Nursing Journal* 29, no. 9 (2014): 302–305, https://doi.org/10.1111/vnj.12175.

4. Ira Byock, *Dying Well: Peace and Possibilities at the End of Life* (Penguin Publishing Group, 1989).

5. Therese Rando, *How to Go on Living When Someone You Love Dies* (Echo Point Books & Media, 2023 [1988]), 90, Kindle.

6. Pauline Boss, *Ambiguous Loss: Learning to Live with Unresolved Grief* (Harvard University Press, 1999), 22, Kindle.

7. Pauline Boss, *Ambiguous Loss*, 603, Kindle.

8. Elisabeth Sifton, *Serenity Prayer: Faith and Politics in Times of Peace and War* (W. W. Norton, 2005).

Chapter 3: Life-Changing, Universe-Shifting Grief

1. Megan Devine, *It's OK That You're Not OK: Meeting Grief and Loss in a Culture That Doesn't Understand* (Sounds True, 2017), 6, Kindle.

2. Karin Brulliard, "A Woman's Dog Died, and Doctors Say Her Heart Literally Broke," *The Washington Post*, October 19, 2017, https://www.washingtonpost.com/news/animalia/wp/2017/10/19/a-womans-dog-died-and-doctors-say-her-heart-literally-broke/.

3. Virginia Hughes, "On Losing a Dog," *National Geographic*, November 21, 2013, https://www.nationalgeographic.com/science/article/on-losing-a-dog?loggedin =true&rnd=1678831310776.

4. Naomi I. Eisenberger, Matthew D. Lieberman, and Kipling D. Williams, "Does Rejection Hurt? An fMRI Study of Social Exclusion," *Science* 302, no. 5643 (2003): 290–292, https://doi.org/10.1126/science.1089134.

5. Joan Didion, *The Year of Magical Thinking* (Vintage International, 2005), 45–46, Kindle.

6. George A. Bonanno, *The Other Side of Sadness: What the New Science of Bereavement Tells Us About Life After Loss* (Basic Books, 2019), 59.

7. Lisa Irish, *Grieving—The Sacred Art: Hope in the Land of Loss* (Turner Publishing Company, 2018), 81, Kindle.

8. Earl A. Grollman, *Straight Talk About Death for Teenagers: How to Cope with Losing Someone You Love* (Beacon Press, 2014), 6.

9. Elisabeth Kübler-Ross, *On Death and Dying* (The Macmillan Company, 1969).

10. Froma Walsh, "Human-Animal Bonds II: The role of Pets in Family Systems and Family Therapy," *Family Process* 48, no. 4 (2009): 481–499, https://doi.org/10.1111/j.1545-5300.2009.01297.x.

Chapter 4: Guilt and Forgiveness

1. Joan Didion, *The Year of Magical Thinking* (Vintage International, 2005), 34, Kindle.

2. John O'Hara, *Appointment in Samarra* (Penguin Publishing, 1963 [1934]).

3. Rami M. Shapiro, *Recovery—The Sacred Art: The Twelve Steps as Spiritual Practice* (SkyLight Paths, 2009), 18.

4. Susan Elizabeth Dawson, "Compassionate Communication: Working with Grief," in *Handbook of Veterinary Communication Skills*, eds. Carol Gray and Jenny Moffett (Blackwell, 2010), 62–99.

5. *Merriam-Webster*, https://www.merriam-webster.com/dictionary/guilt.

6. *Merriam-Webster*, https://www.merriam-webster.com/dictionary/remorse.

7. Caroline Hewson, "Grief for Pets—Part 1: Overview and Some False Assumptions," *Veterinary Nursing Journal* 29, no. 9 (2014): 302–305, https://doi.org/10.1111/vnj.12175.

8. Cori Bussolari et al., "Self-Compassion, Social Constraints, and Psychosocial Outcomes in a Pet Bereavement Sample," *OMEGA—Journal of Death and Dying* 82, no. 3 (2021): 389–408, https://doi.org/10.1177/0030222818814050.

9. Kristen D. Neff, "Self-Compassion: An Alternative Conceptualization of a Healthy Attitude Towards Oneself," *Self and Identity* 2, no. 2 (2003): 85–101, https://doi.org/10.1080/15298860309032; and Kristen D. Neff, "Development and Validation of a Scale to Measure Self-Compassion," *Self and Identity* 2, no. 3 (2003): 223–250, https://doi.org/10.1080/15298860309027.

10. Francis Weller, *The Wild Edge of Sorrow: Rituals of Renewal and the Sacred Work of Grief* (North Atlantic Books, 2015), 151.

Chapter 5: How Culture Shapes Our Grief

1. "Most Popular Pet in Japan: An In-Depth Look at Japanese Pet Culture," PetsCare, https://www.petscare.com/en-sg/news/post/most-popular-pet-japan.

2. Barbara Ambros, *Bones of Contention: Animals and Religion in Contemporary Japan* (University of Hawaii Press, 2012), 1.

3. George A. Bonanno, *The Other Side of Sadness: What the New Science of Bereavement Tells Us About Life After Loss* (Basic Books, 2019), 48.

4. Kathy Charmaz and Melinda Milligan, "Grief," in *The Handbook of the Sociology of Emotions*, eds. Jan Stets and Jonathan H. Turner (Springer Science & Business Media, 2007).

5. Nancy Scheper-Hughes, *Death Without Weeping: The Violence of Everyday Life in Brazil* (University of California Press, 1992), 431.

6. Walter R. Houghton et al., *American Etiquette and Rules of Politeness* (Standard Publishing House, 1889), 273.

7. Geoffrey Gorer, *Death, Grief, and Mourning* (Arno Press, 1965), 12.

8. Megan Devine, *It's OK That You're Not OK: Meeting Grief and Loss in a Culture That Doesn't Understand* (Sounds True, 2017), Introduction, Kindle.

9. Kathy Charmaz and Melinda Milligan, "Grief," 516.

10. American Psychiatric Association, *Diagnostic and Statistical Manual of Mental Disorders* (DSM-5) (American Psychiatric Publishing, 2013).

11. Alan D. Wolfelt, "Grief Is Not a Disorder: My Position on the New 'Prolonged Grief Disorder' Diagnostic Category in the DSM," Center for Grief and Life Transitions, April 11, 2022, https://www.centerforloss.com/2022/04/grief-is-not-a-disorder/.

12. Earl A. Grollman, *Straight Talk About Death for Teenagers: How to Cope with Losing Someone You Love* (Beacon Press, 2014), 6.

13. Packman, Wendy, et al., "Online Survey as Empathic Bridging for the Disenfranchised Grief of Pet Loss," *Omega* 69, no. 4 (2014), 343, https://doi.org/10.2190/OM.69.4.a.

14. Wendy Packman, Betty Carmack, and Rama Ronen, "Therapeutic Implications of Continuing Bonds Expressions Following the Death of a Pet," *Omega* 6, no. 4 (2011): 341, https://doi.org/10.2190/OM.64.4.d.

15. Packman, Wendy, et al., "Online Survey as Empathic Bridging for the Disenfranchised Grief of Pet Loss," *Omega* 69, no. 4 (2014), 350, https://doi.org/10.2190/OM.69.4.a.

16. Charles R. Figley and Robert G. Roop, *Compassion Fatigue in the Animal-Care Community* (Humane Society Press, 2016), ebook, 53.

17. Alisha R. Matte et al., "Exploring Pet Owners' Experiences and Self-Reported Satisfaction and Grief Following Companion Animal Euthanasia," *VetRecord* 187, no. 12 (2020), e122, https://doi.org/10.1136/vr.105734.

18. Elisabeth Kübler-Ross and David Kessler, *On Grief and Grieving: Finding the Meaning of Grief Through the Five Stages of Loss* (Scribner, 2005), xiii.

Chapter 6: Moving On Versus Staying Connected

1. Sigmund Freud, "Mourning and Melancholia," in *The Standard Edition of the Complete Psychological Works of Sigmund Freud*, vol. 14, ed., trans. James Strachey (Basic Books, 1957), 237–260.

2. George A. Bonanno, *The Other Side of Sadness: What the New Science of Bereavement Tells Us About Life After Loss* (Basic Books, 2019), 134.

3. Elisabeth Kübler-Ross and David Kessler, *On Grief and Grieving: Finding the Meaning of Grief Through the Five Stages of Loss* (Scribner, 2005), 7.

4. Elisabeth Kübler-Ross and David Kessler, *On Grief and Grieving*, 24.

5. J. William Worden, *Grief Counseling and Grief Therapy: A Handbook for the Mental Health Practitioner*, 1st ed. (Springer, 1982).

6. J. William Worden, *Grief Counseling and Grief Therapy*, 15.

7. J. William Worden, *Grief Counseling and Grief Therapy: A Handbook for the Mental Health Practitioner*, 4th ed. (Springer, 2008), xiv.

8. Alan D. Wolfelt, *Companioning the Bereaved: A Soulful Guide for Caregivers* (Companion Press, 2006).

9. Dennis Klass, Phyllis R. Silverman, and Steven Nickman, eds., *Continuing Bonds: New Understandings of Grief* (Taylor & Francis, 1996).

10. Dennis Klass, Phyllis R. Silverman, and Steven Nickman, eds., *Continuing Bonds*.

11. Wendy Packman, Betty Carmack, and Rama Ronen, "Therapeutic Implications of Continuing Bonds Expressions Following the Death of a Pet," *Omega* 6, no. 4 (2011): 335–356, https://doi.org/10.2190/OM.64.4.d.

12. The term *generativity* was introduced in 1959 by psychoanalyst Erik Erikson in Identity and the Life Cycle (W. W. Norton & Co., 1959). Erikson used the term specifically to denote "a concern for establishing and guiding the next generation." Erikson's use of the term assumes that all human beings seek to reproduce themselves biologically. He noted that "although there are people who, from misfortune or because of special and genuine gifts in other directions, do not apply this drive to offspring but to other forms of altruistic concern and of creativity, which may absorb their kind of parental responsibility" (p. 103). I use the term more broadly to denote people's desire to serve as a positive or "generative" force in the world, and I tie it specifically to the way people respond to the experience of losing an animal companion.

13. George A. Bonanno, *The Other Side of Sadness: What the New Science of Bereavement Tells Us About Life After Loss* (Basic Books, 2019).

14. George A. Bonanno, *The Other Side of Sadness*, 73.

15. Robert E. Gierka, "A Case Study of Veterinary Technology Students' Experience of Continuing Human-Animal Bonds," North Carolina State University, January 2015, https://www.academia.edu/10130134/A_Case_Study_of_Veterinary_Technology_Students_Experience_of_Continuing_Human_Animal_Bonds.

16. Wendy Packman, Betty Carmack, and Rama Ronen, "Therapeutic Implications of Continuing Bonds Expressions Following the Death of a Pet," *Omega* 6, no. 4 (2011): 348, https://doi.org/10.2190/OM.64.4.d.

17. Wendy Packman, Betty Carmack, and Rama Ronen, "Therapeutic Implications of Continuing Bonds Expressions Following the Death of a Pet," 344.

18. Pamela A. Hays, *Addressing Cultural Complexities in Practice: A Framework for Clinicians and Counselors* (American Psychological Association, 2007).

19. Kate Anne Avis, Margaret Stroebe, and Henk Schut, "Stages of Grief Portrayed on the Internet: A Systematic Analysis and Critical Appraisal," *Frontiers in Psychology* 2 (December 2, 2021), https://pubmed.ncbi.nlm.nih.gov/34925174/.

20. David B. Feldman, "Why the Five Stages of Grief Are Wrong," *Psychology Today*, July 7, 2017, https://www.psychologytoday.com/us/blog/supersurvivors/201707/why-the-five-stages-grief-are-wrong.

Chapter 7: Coping with Loss

1. The Ohio State University Veterinary Medical Center, "Coping with the Loss of a Pet: A Guide for Adults, Children and Surviving Animals," PDF download, retrieved March 25, 2025, https://vmc.vet.osu.edu/sites/default/files/documents/coping_with_loss_brochure_2024_web.pdf.

2. Jessica K. Walker, Natalie K. Waran, and Clive J. C. Phillips, "Owners' Perceptions of Their Animal's Behavioural Response to the Loss of an Animal Companion," *Animals* 6, no. 11 (2016): 68, https://doi.org/10.3390/ani6110068.

3. Ellen Lindell and Lynn Buzhardt, "Helping Your Grieving Pet," VCA Hospitals, retrieved March 23, 2025, https://vcahospitals.com/know-your-pet/helping-your-grieving-pet.

4. Trisha Walsh, "When You Cry for Whatever Reasons, Do Your Pets Seem to Sense You Are Sad and Try to Comfort You?," Quora, retrieved March 25, 2025, https://www.quora.com/When-you-cry-for-whatever-reason-do-your-pets-seem-to-sense-you-are-sad-and-try-to-comfort-you. To access this article, log into Quora and search for the article's title.

5. Terry L. Martin and Wen-Chi Wang, "A Pilot Study of the Development of a Tool to Measure Instrumental and Intuitive Styles of Grieving," *Omega* 53, no. 4 (2006): 263–278, https://doi.org/10.2190/Y888-0T65-7T87-8136; and Kenneth J. Doka and Terry L. Martin, "Grieving Styles: Gender and Grief," *Grief Matters: The Australian Journal of Grief and Bereavement* 14, no. 2, (2011): 42–45, https://search.informit.org/doi/10.3316/informit.339916590087229.

6. Lori R. Kogan et al., "Pet Death and Owners' Memorialization Choices," *Illness, Crisis & Loss* 32, no. 2 (2022), https://doi.org/10.1177/10541373221143046.

7. Gary Kurz, *Cold Noses at the Pearly Gates: A Book of Hope for Those Who Have Lost a Pet* (Citadel Press, 2013), 3, Kindle.

8. Andrew Newberg and Mark Robert Waldman, *How God Changes Your Brain: Breakthrough Findings from a Leading Neuroscientist* (Random House, 2010), 149.

9. Nour Abdullah, "The Scientific Effects of Gratitude: A Review," *Journal of Positive Psychology and Wellbeing* 7, no. 3 (2023): 192–205, https://journalppw.com/index.php/jppw/article/view/17539.

10. Elisabeth Kübler-Ross and David Kessler, *On Grief and Grieving: Finding the Meaning of Grief Through the Five Stages of Loss* (Scribner, 2005), 63.

Chapter 8: Making Meaning of Loss

1. Stephen R. Shuchter and Sidney Zisook, "The Course of Normal Grief," in *Handbook of Bereavement: Theory, Research, and Intervention*, eds. Margaret S. Stroebe, Wolfgang Stroebe, and Robert O. Hansson (Cambridge University Press, 1993), 23–43.

2. Jack Mezirow and Associates, *Fostering Critical Reflection in Adulthood* (Jossey-Bass Publishers, 1990).

3. Jack Mezirow and Associates, *Fostering Critical Reflection in Adulthood*, 1.

4. Julie Stern, "What Is Schema? How Do We Help Students Build It?" *Education Week*, October 20, 2019, https://www.edweek.org/teaching-learning/opinion-what-is-schema-how-do-we-help-students-build-it/2019/10.

5. Mary-Frances O'Connor and Saren H. Seeley, "Grieving as a Form of Learning: Insights from Neuroscience Applied to Grief and Loss," *Current Opinion in Psychology* 20, no. 43 (2021): 317–322, https://doi.org/10.1016/j.copsyc.2021.08.019.

6. Claudia Christine Wolf, "Grief Is a Learning Experience," *Scientific American*, February 27, 2024, https://www.scientificamerican.com/article/how-the-brain-copes-with-grief/#:~:text=Grieving%20can%20be%20thought%20of%20as%20a,instead%20of%20a%20married%20person%2C%20for%20example.&text=-Being%20very%20isolated%20also%20seems%20to%20predict%20poorer%20outcomes%20in%20grieving.

7. Claudia Christine Wolf, "Grief Is a Learning Experience."

8. Jack Mezirow and Associates, *Fostering Critical Reflection in Adulthood* (Jossey-Bass Publishers, 1990), 4.

9. Jack Mezirow and Associates, *Fostering Critical Reflection in Adulthood*, 1.

10. Wendy Packman et al., "Online Survey as Empathic Bridging for the Disenfranchised Grief of Pet Loss," *Omega* 69 (2014) 333–356, https://doi.org/10.2190/om.69.4.a.

11. Wendy Packman et al., "Online Survey as Empathic Bridging for the Disenfranchised Grief of Pet Loss," 343.

12. Wendy Packman et al., "Online Survey as Empathic Bridging for the Disenfranchised Grief of Pet Loss," 343.

13. Wendy Packman et al., "Online Survey as Empathic Bridging for the Disenfranchised Grief of Pet Loss," 349.

Chapter 9: Generativity

1. "The Rainbow Bridge" poem is credited to Edna Clyne-Rekhy, a Scottish artist and animal lover who wrote the poem shortly after the loss of her dog Major in 1959. For more information, see Paul Koudounaris's article "The Rainbow Bridge: The True Story Behind History's Most Influential Piece of Animal Mourning Literature," The Order of the Good Death, February 9, 2023, https://www.orderofthegooddeath.com/article/the-rainbow-bridge-the-true-story-behind-historys-most-influential-piece-of-animal-mourning-literature/.

2. Elisabeth Kübler-Ross and David Kessler, *On Grief and Grieving: Finding the Meaning of Grief Through the Five Stages of Loss* (Scribner, 2014).

3. Elisabeth Kübler-Ross and David Kessler, *On Grief and Grieving*, 212.

4. Elisabeth Kübler-Ross and David Kessler, *On Grief and Grieving*, 216.

Chapter 10: Crafting Your Sacred Story: Connecting and Coping

1. Pamela A. Hays, *Addressing Cultural Complexities in Practice: A Framework for Clinicians and Counselors* (American Psychological Association, 2007).

2. Lodro Rinzler, as quoted in Liza Kindred, *Eff This! Meditation: 108 Tips, Tricks, and Ideas for When You're Feeling Anxious, Stressed Out, or Overwhelmed* (Rock Point, 2019).

3. Janet Conner, *Writing Down Your Soul: How to Activate and Listen to the Extraordinary Voice Within* (Mango Media, 2021).

4. Janet Conner, *Writing Down Your Soul*, 7.

5. Janet Conner, *Writing Down Your Soul*, 7.

6. Janet Conner explores the science that supports the power of writing to help us gain new insights in a chapter titled "Why Write?" in *Writing Down Your Soul*.

Selected Bibliography

Ambros, Barbara. *Bones of Contention: Animals and Religion in Contemporary Japan*. University of Hawaii Press, 2012.

Bekoff, Marc. *The Emotional Lives of Animals: A Leading Scientist Explores Animal Joy, Sorrow, and Empathy—and Why They Matter*. New World Library, 2010.

Bonanno, George A. *The Other Side of Sadness: What the New Science of Bereavement Tells Us About Life After Loss*. Basic Books, 2019.

Boss, Pauline. *Ambiguous Loss: Learning to Live with Unresolved Grief*. Harvard University Press, 1999.

Bussolari, Cori, et al. "Self-Compassion, Social Constraints, and Psychosocial Outcomes in a Pet Bereavement Sample." *OMEGA Journal of Death and Dying* 82, no. 3 (2021): 389–408. http://dx.doi.org/10.1177/0030222818814050.

Byock, Ira. *Dying Well: Peace and Possibilities at the End of Life*. Penguin Publishing Group, 1989.

Charmaz, Kathy, and Melinda Milligan. "Grief." In *The Handbook of the Sociology of Emotions*, edited by Jan Stets and Jonathan H. Turner. Springer Science & Business Media, 2007.

Devine, Megan. *It's OK That You're Not OK: Meeting Grief and Loss in a Culture That Doesn't Understand*. Sounds True, 2017.

Didion, Joan. *The Year of Magical Thinking*. Vintage International, 2005.

Freud, Sigmund. "Mourning and Melancholia." In *The Standard Edition of the Complete Psychological Works of Sigmund Freud*, Vol. 14. Edited and translated by James Strachey. Basic Books, 1957.

Hewson, Caroline. "Grief for Pets—Part 1: Overview and Some False Assumptions." *Veterinary Nursing Journal* 29, no. 9 (2014): 302–305. https://doi.org/10.1111/vnj.12175.

Irish, Lisa. *Grieving—The Sacred Art: Hope in the Land of Loss*. Turner Publishing Company, 2018.

Katz, Jon. *Soul of a Dog: Reflections on the Spirits of the Animals of Bedlam Farm*. Random House, 2009.

Klass, Dennis, Phyllis R. Silverman, and Steven Nickman, eds. *Continuing Bonds: New Understandings of Grief*. Taylor & Francis, 1996.

Knapp, Caroline. *Pack of Two: The Intricate Bond between People and Dogs*. Random House, 2010.

Kübler-Ross, Elisabeth. *On Death and Dying*. The Macmillan Company, 1969.

Kübler-Ross, Elisabeth, and David Kessler. *On Grief and Grieving: Finding the Meaning of Grief Through the Five Stages of Loss.* Scribner, 2005.

Kwong, Marilyn J. and Kim Bartholomew. "Not Just a Dog": An Attachment Perspective on Relationships with Assistance Dogs." *Attachment & Human Development* 13, no. 5 (2011): 422. https://doi.org/10.1080/14616734.2011.584410.

Melson, Gail. *Why the Wild Things Are: Animals in the Lives of Children.* Harvard University Press, 2009.

Mezirow, Jack, and Associates. *Fostering Critical Reflection in Adulthood.* Jossey-Bass Publishers, 1990.

Packman, Wendy, et al. "Online Survey as Empathic Bridging for the Disenfranchised Grief of Pet Loss." *Omega* 69 (2014): 333–356. https://doi.org/10.2190/om.69.4.a.

Packman, Wendy, Betty Carmack, and Rama Ronen. "Therapeutic Implications of Continuing Bonds Expressions Following the Death of a Pet." *Omega* 6, no. 4 (2011): 335–356. https://doi.org/10.2190/OM.64.4.d.

Rando, Therese. *How to Go on Living When Someone You Love Dies.* Echo Point Books & Media, 2023 [1988].

Schaffer, Michael. *One Nation Under Dog: Adventures in the New World of Prozac-Popping Puppies, Dog-Park Politics, and Organic Pet Food.* Holt, 2009.

Shapiro, Rami M. *Recovery—the Sacred Art: The Twelve Steps as Spiritual Practice.* SkyLight Paths, 2009.

Walsh, Froma. "Human-Animal Bonds II: The Role of Pets in Family Systems and Family Therapy." *Family Process* 48, no. 4 (2009). http://dx.doi.org/10.1111/j.1545-5300.2009.01297.x.

Weller, Francis. *The Wild Edge of Sorrow: Rituals of Renewal and the Sacred Work of Grief.* North Atlantic Books, 2015.

Wolfelt, Alan D. *Companioning the Bereaved: A Soulful Guide for Caregivers.* Companion Press, 2006.

Worden, J. William. *Grief Counseling and Grief Therapy: A Handbook for the Mental Health Practitioner*, 4th edition. Springer, 2009.

Index

3 Chaplain Cs Method of Storytelling 158

Abiding Ties Pet Loss Support Group 132
abuse, animal 7
acceptance of death: vs. feelings about loss 53; in five stages of grief model 53
addiction as factor in experience of grief 55
adult education and meaning-making 134
afterlife: religious and spiritual traditions 139
age of pet and experience of grief 54
alienation 139
ambiguous loss 37–40
Ambros, Barbara 70
American culture; as grief avoidant xxi
American Psychiatric Association (APA) 75
anger: ambiguous loss and 38; as common 60–61; denial and 52; emotional oscillation in grief and 48; in five stages of grief model 52; intense grief and 43; powerlessness and 60–62, 83; questions for 83; sudden loss and 36, 138
animals as teachers: authentic self and 8–9; forgiveness and 7–8; joy and 14; living in the moment 14–16; love and 4–7, 18–20; nurturing and 18–20; overview of 3–4; physical touch and 12–14; questions for 23; traditional knowledge 3; trust and 8; unconditional love and 4–7
Anna (vet tech student) 94
anticipatory grief 29–31, 51–53

anxiety: about death 62; human disorder 66, 116; of pets 109; separation anxiety 109
"Appointment in Samarra" (Maugham) 61
atonement 150
attachment theory 13
attachment to pets; as factor in grief experience 54–55
authentic self: animals as teachers and 8–9

baby boomers, pet-keeping trends 20
bargaining in five stages of grief model 53
Barkley (dog) 144
behavioral issues (animals): abuse and 7; animal grief and 109; dementia and 38; as factor in experience of grief 55; relinquishment and ambiguous loss 38
Bekoff, Marc 7
Bella (labradoodle) 34
Bella (terrier mix) 112
Bill and Sammy 88–89
Blackie (rabbit) 147–149
blame 81
Bonanno, George 71, 90, 95, 98
bonding; petting and 12
Boss, Pauline 37, 39
brain: cognition and mental fog 46, 59; loss and learning centers of 136
Briggs, Dwight 57–60, 63, 65
broken heart syndrome 45
Bryan and Ringo 30, 44, 97
bucket lists 116
Buddhism: forgiveness and 7; living in the moment and 16

burials and funerals: author and Peanut 28; as coping strategy 114, 119; duration of grief and 74; generativity and 151
busyness 50
Byock, Ira 34

caregiver identity 107
care of pets: constancy and 11; nurturing and 19, 20
cats: and Dwight Biggs 57–60; author and Peanut 27–29; dementia and 38; grief of 71
Celeste (vet tech student) 64, 150
chaplaincy. *See* veterinary chaplaincy
Charmaz, Kathy 72, 75
children: confiding in pets 6; percentage living with pets 16; pets as 18–20; play with pets 17–19; role of pets during hard times 5–6; touch deprivation and 13; unexpressed grief 89
Christianity: forgiveness and 7; pets and the afterlife 139; suffering and 139
Cline, Cindy 70
cognitive schema 135–136
Colleen (vet tech student); Pretzel and 17
communicating with animals: continuing bonds expressions 93; emotional 9–10; euthanasia decisions 32, 34–35; eye contact and 33; language of the heart 9–10
communicating with humans and end-of-life conversations 34
compassion: self-compassion 66–67
complex emotion, grief as 45
complicated grief 75
connection: creating sacred stories 159
Conner, Janet 165
constancy of pets 10–12

continuing bond expressions 93–95, 127, 133; benefits of 95–97; distressing aspects of 97–98; passage of time and 97–98
continuing bonds understanding of grief 92–97, 127, 133
control, loss of: coping strategies 114; powerlessness and 60–62
coping with loss: continuing bonds understanding of grief and 95; daily routines and 107–108; self-compassion and 66; strategies for xx, 113–125; sudden loss and capacity to cope 36
cortisol 12
Coulson, Bob 150
creative work as coping strategy 114, 121, 147, 151
creativity and inner voice 165
crying 43
C-tactile afferents 12
culture: meaning-making and 135; social constructionism 71

Daisy (hamster) 5
Dare (dog) 6, 17–18
death: powerlessness and 61; spiritual growth and personal transformation 151
dementia, pets with 38
denial: in five stages of grief model 52; unavoidability of grief and 50
depression: as factor in experience of grief 55; in five stages of grief model 53; medication for 75; self-compassion and 66
DeRosa, Mary 118
detachment models of grief 90, 91–96
Devine, Megan 43, 73
Didion, Joan 46, 59
disenfranchisement of pet loss 78
disorienting dilemmas 135, 139, 153
Divine Voice 165

dogs 109: as partners in travel and adventure 16; dementia and 38; grief of 71, 109; hospice service 9
donations 118
Duke, Karen xv, xvii, 36, 69, 131

Elaine and Harvey 41–43, 77, 98, 137–139
emotions: acceptance vs. feelings about loss 53; decline in pet's health and emotional roller coaster 52; gender and emotional expression 55; oscillation of 48; taking time to feel 49
emotions, animal: communication and 9–10
emotions, human: creating sacred stories and 161
empathy 66
endorphins 12
ethics and veterinary workers xxiii
euthanasia: grief of other pets and 110; guilt and 33; uncertainty and 28, 30–34
exercise, physical 115
extraordinary experiences 99–101
eye contact: emotional connection and 10
eye contact and communicating with animals 33

five stages model of grief 51–53, 91; as a roadmap for grief 103; popularity of 102
forgiveness: and guilt or remorse 65–67; animals as teachers 7–8; spiritual traditions and 7
Frank (vet tech student) 5, 11, 19, 96, 142
Freddie (cat) 34, 50, 141
Freud, Sigmund 9, 90
fun: John and Dare 17–18
fur baby term 18

future: animal perceptions of 15; human perceptions of 15

geese 46
gender: expression of grief and 73; as factor in experience of grief 55; isolation and 55
generativity 95, 144–152, 153; as a continuing bond expression 95
Goathouse Refuge 87
Gorer, Geoffrey 73
gratitude xxi, 121, 153
Great Books Foundation xv
grief: American culture as grief avoidant xxi; as complex emotion 45; continuing bonds understanding of 92–97, 127, 133; creating sacred stories and xxii, 165; detachment models of 90–92; duration of 49, 74, 81; five stages model of 90–92; for sacred places xxiii; for wild animals xxiii; four tasks model of 92; institutional disenfranchisement and 78; intensity of as disorienting 140; lack of social support and 78–79; as nonlinear process xix, 91; physical manifestations of 42, 43, 45–51; self-care tips 165; six needs of mourning 92; as spiritual experience xx–xxii; as unavoidable 76; unexpressed 89
grief literacy 80–82
grief of animals: as social phenomenon 71; of surviving pets 109–111
grieving styles 114
Grollman, Earl 50
growth, potential for xxi, 134, 151

guilt: ambiguous loss and 38; atonement and 64; as common experience when a pet is lost 59–61; continuing bonds expressions 98; creating sacred stories and 161; euthanasia and 33; generative acts and 150; intense grief and 43; magical thinking and 59; powerlessness and 60–62, 83; prayer and 66; questions for 83; remorse and 65; rituals and 66; self-compassion and 66–67; sudden loss and 36, 65, 138; term 64; writing a letter to a pet 65

Harvey (dog) 41–43, 77, 98, 137–139
Hays, Pamela A. 101, 159
healing: relationships and 164
health, animal and healing modalities 14
health, human: animals in health care settings 9, 12; effect of grief on 46; healing quality of animals 9, 12; medicalization of grief 75, 116; profundity of grief and 54, 55
health, pets: costs and 29, 32; dementia and 38; denial of 52; emotional roller coaster and 52; isolation and 30; monitoring 31; uncertainty and 27–29
Heart Animals (Gierka & Duke) 96, 101, 157, 166
help: accepting 58; helping others and generativity 144–152; helping others as coping strategy 118
helplessness: questions for 83; uncertainty and 28, 37
Holly (dog) 104–106, 122
hope: denial and hopelessness 52; resiliency and 44
hospice, service dogs in 9
Houghton, Walter R. 73
human-animal bond xiii, xv, xvi
humanity and self-compassion 67

identity: authentic self and animals as teachers 8–9; caregiver identity 107; sacred stories and xvi; in six needs model of grief 92; spirituality and xxi
Indigenous traditions 3
inflammation 46
innocents, suffering of 139
instrumental grieving style 115
intuitive grieving style 115
Irish, Lisa xxi, 48
isolation: coping strategies 119; decline in pet's health and 30; dismissal of grief and 80; gender and 55; profundity of grief and 54
Izzy (dog) 9

Jasper (Chinese moon bear) 7
Jesus 7
Jofi (dog) 9
John (vet tech student) 6, 17–18
journaling 105, 121
joy 14
Just an Animal (Gierka & Duke) 48, 78, 158

Katz, Jon 9
Kelly (vet tech student) 96; Daisy and 5; Zuzu and 10
Kessler, David 91
Kimmerer, Robin Wall 3
Klass, Dennis 93
Knapp, Caroline 12
Kübler-Ross, Elisabeth: Blackie and 147–149; five stages of grief model 51–53, 91–96; grief literacy and 81; helping others focus 149; and misinterpretation of five stages model 91; on storytelling 123
Kurz, Gary 120

Lake Lure 144–147

learning: adult education and 134; from continuing bonds expressions 93; Linda and Maggie 132–133; transformative 137–142
Lewis, C. S. xix
Lillian (vet tech student) 34, 50, 141
Lindemann, Erich 29
living in the moment 14–16, 138
longevity of animal-human relationship; benefits of 11; Frank and Muppet 11
lost, feeling xix
loudest silence 106
love: animals as teachers and 18–20; continuing bonds understanding of grief 93–97; nonjudgmental/ unconditional 42
love, nonjudgmental/unconditional: animal teachers and 4–7
loyalty and human security 11

Maggie (dog) 100, 132–133
magical thinking 59
Marks, Steven 32
Martka, Shirley 37
massage 14
McCool: Dean 104–105; Kim 104–113, 122
meals 115
meaning and meaning-making: adult education and 134; defined 134; disorienting dilemmas 135, 139–140, 153; from loss 131–165; questions for 153; in six needs model 92; transformative learning 137–142; writing and 165
meaning reformation 141
medicalization of grief 75–77, 116
meditation: Divine Voice and 165
Melson, Gail 16
memory: continuing bonds expressions 93, 133
memory, animal 15

memory, human:; reconstructing memories of pets 164
mental fog 46
mental health: as factor in experience of grief 55; medicalization of grief 75–77, 116; medications and 116; self-compassion and 66; stigma of mental illness 76
mental health practitioners: lack of education in pet loss 78
Mercedes (dog) 14, 117
messages from deceased pets 112
Mezirow, Jack 134–135
millennials, pet-keeping trends 19
Millie (dog) 13
Milligan, Melinda 72, 75
mindfulness 67
minimizing/dismissing grief: in American culture xxi, 77; as disorienting dilemma 139; focus on moving on 89–92; hiding grief from other pets 111; managing 47–49; unexpressed grief and 89
Mixon; Alan 112; Sandra 112
Molly (dog) 144
moment, living in 138
Moore, Linda 100, 131–134
mourning etiquette 73
Muppet (cat) 5, 11, 19, 96

nature: inner voice and 165
need to be needed 18
Neff, Kristen D. 66
Nickman, Steven 93
nirvana 16
nurturing: animals as teachers and 18–20; need to be needed and 18; purpose and 18, 20

O'Connor, Mary-Frances 136
Oscar (cat) 27
oxytocin 12

pain: petting/touch and 12

pain, human: intense grief and 43; physical manifestations of grief 46; in six needs model 92
pain, pet and quality of life 31
past: animal perceptions of 15; human perceptions of 15
pathological grief 75
Peanut (cat) 27–29
personality, as factor in experience of grief 55
Pet Chaplain Learning Series: contemplative practice and xvi; geographical limitations of research xiv; overview xiii–xvii
Pet Chaplain organization xiii
pet keeping in Japan 69
pet loss: institutional disenfranchisement and 78–79; lack of social support and 78; online support for 79; veterinary clinics and 79. *See also* grief
pet loss support groups 123; author's xiv; benefits of 124
pets: authenticity of 8; as children 18–20; constancy of 10–12; generational trends in pet-keeping 19; getting new pet 107, 112–113; grief of surviving pets 109–111; as a healing presence 9–10; hiding grief from 111; importance of touch and 12–14; as innocents 64; joy and play 16–18; and living in the moment 14–16
physical manifestations of grief 42, 43, 45–51
physical sensations and continuing bonds expressions 93
physical touch: animals as teachers and 12–14; benefits of 12–14; safe havens and 13; touch and healing modalities for pets 14; touch deprivation 13
Pixie (dog) 150
play: children and 17–19
positive feelings during grief 48, 91

possessions, pet's: continuing bonds expressions 93; coping strategies and 107, 108
Posttraumatic growth 141
powerlessness and guilt 60–62, 83
prayer: inner voice and 165
Prem, Fran 33
preplanning for a pet's death 116
presence: continuing bonds expressions 93, 96; coping strategies and 121; emptiness and 106
present: animal perceptions of 15; human perceptions of 16
Pretzel (dog) 17
prior experience of death: as factor in grief experience 56
prolonged grief disorder (PGD) 76
purpose in nurturing 18, 20

quality of life, assessing 31
Queenie (dog) 166

Rachel (vet tech student) 17, 39
Raffi (dog) 17, 33, 39
"The Rainbow Bridge" poem 144
rainbow bridge at Lake Lure 144–147
Rambo (dog) 64, 150
Rando, Therese 36
Reiki 14
relationships, human: complexity of 4; dismissal of grief 139; healing and 164; sharing stories and 123
relief 48
religion: forgiveness and 7
religion and spiritual traditions: afterlife and 120, 139; disorienting dilemmas and 139; grief rituals 119; religious disenfranchisement 140
relinquishment of pets: ambiguous loss and 38–40; denial and 52; as factor in experience of grief 55
remorse: term 64. *See also* guilt
rescue work: forgiveness by animals and 7

resilience: hope and 44; sudden loss and 42
Ringo (dog) 30, 44
Rinzler, Lodro 164
Rodriguez, Cindi 14, 117
routines, daily 107–108
rumination: as common 59–61; coping strategies 114, 123

sacred stories: about xiv, 157; continuing bonds expressions and 96; coping strategies and xx; exercises xv; identity and xvi; Linda and Maggie 132–133; questions for xvi; sharing xvi
sacred story project 157–167, 158–167; brainstorming for 163; defining your guiding purpose 162; immersive writing exercise 165–167; revisiting your past 164; visual aids 164; writing from your heart 165; writing prompts 160–161
safe havens 13
Sammy (dog) 88–89
Sarah (dog) 36
Scarpa, Siglinda 87
Scheper-Hughes, Nancy 72
Scooter (cat) 57, 63
Scott, Christine 110
searching behavior 110
self-care 115; tips for 160
self-compassion 66–67
self-discovery exercises and practices: about xv; immersive writing exercise 165–166; questions 83; sacred stories, creating xv; self-care tips 165; self-reflection and meaning-making 134
self-forgiveness: guilt and 65–68; self-compassion and 66–67; spiritual or religious reflection and 66; through rituals 65; through volunteer activities 65
self-improvement 67

self-kindness 66
senior citizens and pets 20
sensing a deceased pet's presence 99, 127
separation anxiety 109
Serpell, James 6
service animals, relinquishment of 38
shame 76, 80
Shapiro, Rami 63
shimmering moments 101, 159
shrines and memorials: continuing bonds expressions 93; as coping strategy 107, 112, 114, 118; generativity and 151; pet's possessions in 108
Shuchter, Stephen R. 133
silence, loudest 106
Silverman, Phyllis 93
six needs model of grief 92
sleep issues 43
social constructionism 71
spirituality: diversity of practices xvi; grief as spiritual process xx–xxii; identity and xxi; messages from deceased pets 112; spiritual amalgamations xvi
Stanley (dog) 41, 137
Stella (dog) 113
storytelling: as a continuing bond expression 94; as coping strategy 114; questions for 83, 153
stress: physical manifestations of grief and 46; profundity of grief and concurrent stressors 54, 55
styles, grieving 114
sudden loss: continuing bonds expressions 98; Elaine and Harvey 42–43, 98, 137–139; experience of grief and 55; uncertainty and 28, 35–37
support groups 123–124, 132, 151
synchronicity moments 159

time 49, 74, 81; creating sacred stories and 166; exercises and 166; human vs. animal perceptions of 14–16
transformative learning 137–142
trauma and hard times: animals as refuge during 5; John 17–18; Kelly 5
trust: animals as teachers and 8; constancy and 11; petting and 12

uncertainty: ambiguous loss and 37–40; decline and illness 27–29; euthanasia and 28, 30–34; helplessness and 28, 37; questions for 83; sudden loss and 28, 35–37; treatment 28; unpredictability of grief 48
uniqueness of individual grief 54–63
veterinary care: client support and 79; denial and 52; preplanning for a pet's death and 116; uncertainty and 28
veterinary chaplaincy xxii; online course xv
veterinary workers: continuing bonds expressions 96; ethics of treatment xxiii; grief of job xxiii
vet techs: as study participants xv; title xv
visual aids and sacred stories 164
voice: Divine Voice 165; writing and 165
volunteering 118
vulnerability 8, 43, 56

Wald, Amy 144–146
Weller, Francis 67
Wolfelt, Alan D. 76, 92
wonder 18
Worden, J. William 92
work: generative acts and 150; grief dismissal and 81; grief support and 74; struggles with 77, 139
writing exercise 166–167

writing from the scar 164

Zisook, Sidney 133
Zuzu (dog) 10